The Life Of A locomotive Engineer

From Steam To Diesel

By J. O. Young

 www.trafford.com

North America & international
toll-free: 844-688-6899 (USA & Canada)
fax: 812 355 4082

1

Contents

Acknowledgement

I wish to thank my wife for her help in getting this project started, for without it, this book would probably have never been written. I would also like to thank the Richmond Palladium for the use of their pictures of the wreck that took place on the railroad bridge just east of Richmond, as well as fellow employees who also donated pictures.

1920s &1930s

Effects Of Depression

Life began for me near Hinton, West Virginia on June 8, 1928 in the New River Valley of the Southern Appalachian Mountains. At this time my Dad was serving his apprenticeship for a position as machinist at the C&O shops in Hinton, and we were living in a small five room cottage about two miles from town. This house we were living in belonged to my granddad, Ed Young. In March of 1931, he traded it for a house just across the river from town. Though I was only three years old when we moved there, I still remember a few things that happened at the time. Such as my mom's sister chasing me around the house. She was about thirteen and lived with my grandparents on the farm. Not long after that, she was building a fire outside to boil some clothes in doing laundry, when by mistake she poured gasoline on the fire instead of kerosene. The gas can exploded giving her severe burns. About three days later she died. I also remember looking out the window of the front door during a flood and seeing the body of a man floating down the river. It was also at this time that the depression began to take effect. My dad was laid off from the railroad and as yet hadn't found a job. We had a Model A Roadster, and I remember two men, dressed in overcoats, coming to the door and asking for the keys. My dad was unable to make payments on it, so they drove it away, and I never saw it again. That was about 1931, and we never had another car until 1937.My granddad worked in the C&O shops also and lived on a farm about a mile away. In October 1933, my granddad was still working, and my dad was out of work. We traded living places, so my dad could work the farm. Times on the farm during the depression were not so bad, though I've heard my mom say I got repainted toys for Christmas during this time.

Wrong Place Wrong Time

One sunshiny morning, my mom sent my sister, who was about ten years old, and I, about five, to my aunt's house who lived about a half mile farther up the valley. To get there, we took a path along the creek, which was a short cut. At one point along this path there was a huge boulder. From this boulder there was a good view of the county road, which was approximately 300 yards away and across the creek. Not until we arrived at my aunt's house did we learn that a man was behind the big rock that we had walked by. He had shot a man off his horse, which was going down the road, and killed him. He must have shot him a few minutes before we got there since we didn't hear, or possibly notice, the shot. Nevertheless, we had walked between the two men. This was in the early thirties, and though only a few people still rode horses, this man, a local lawyer, was riding one.

Only One Boss

One time my dad and I were hauling fifty gallon barrels of water on a sled being pulled by a mule. I was standing on the sled behind the barrels. The mule stopped, and when he started again, he gave a jerk that sent the barrel and me; I was standing behind, off the sled. Luckily, I fell into a huge rut in the dirt road that prevented the barrel from doing a number on me. However, I did receive an instant bath.

The mule we were using on the farm was a worker, but was well past his prime. I later

Learned my Dad had been in town previously and overheard a conversation between two men, one being an older man. The older man told his friend he had a big mule at home he didn't know what to do with. He said his son use to work him, but he had left for service, and he couldn't do anything with him. In fact, he was afraid to let him out of the barn. My Dad told him, "I have an older mule at home that is a good worker. I'll swap you even for him." After the swap, my Dad brought the mule home, put him in the barn, and left him for a couple of days. He was one big mule. One morning he put the harness and driving lines on the mule and took him on top of the mountain, in back of our farm, to get a load of logs for firewood. In about two hours they were back. My Dad unhooked the logs, turned the mule around and said, "get up mule," with the idea of going back for another load of logs. Well the mule decided he had already had enough of the logging business for the day and wouldn't budge. I knew right away this mule was in trouble. He was about to learn something I had known for a long time. There was only one boss on this farm. My Dad was it. No mule, regardless of size, was going to change that. I went up on the bank nearby and waited to see the show, for I knew there was going to be one. The mule had a halter as well as a bridle on. My Dad led him over to a fence, took off the bridle and tied him to the fence with the halter. He then took the bridle into the barn. A short time later, he came out carrying the bridle and a piece of cable about five feet long. He had wrapped a fine wire around the bit on the bridle. After putting the bridle back on, he turned the mule around and said, "Get up mule." Again he didn't move. That was the mule's second mistake. My Dad hit him with the cable at least two times before he had time to move. The mule then took off up the mountain running with my Dad holding on to the reins and running after him. There after the mule never gave my Dad any more trouble and he proved to be a very good worker.

Things That Happened On Granddad Lilly's Farm

When I was very young, my family would go to my mom's parents, who lived about ten miles from Hinton, on a farm. My oldest memory is of me riding my tricycle out near the tool shed on this farm. I met up with a mother hen and about ten baby chicks. Instead of going around, I went right through the middle of them. I haven't a clue as to why I did that. However, about that time my grandmother came on the scene. Being a little upset with me, she told my mother, who first gave me a lecture and was then about to give me another lesson with a paddle as well. Grandmother talked her out of it. Even though I know I well deserved it.

In 1927, my granddad bought a new 1927 Chevy truck. Seven years later, he bought another new truck and like all practicing Hillbillies, he just left the old one set out by the barn. I probably doubled the mileage on that old truck by playing in it every time we went there. When we moved to the coalfields from Hinton, I would occasionally go in the summer and stay awhile. Usually, when I was there, one of my cousins would come and stay also. One day five or six of us, including my uncles and granddad, were hoeing out a cornfield. My cousin Todd and I decided we would pay a visit to an apple tree located in the cornfield. When we had our fill of apples, we went back to get our hoes and couldn't find them. Though we didn't loose them intentionally, we were forever accused of it. Our uncles never let us forget about that one.

Another time in this same field that was now planted in cabbage, I was standing near my granddad's 1937 pickup, when my granddad walked up and said, "Jack, can you drive?" I said, "Yes." Being eight years old, I actually had never driven anything, but I thought from watching my dad and uncles drive I would be able to do it. In his younger days, my granddad had been a school- teacher, but he had lost his eyesight, and now he could only tell night from day. He got in the truck and said " OK, take me down to the fence." (The fence was a rail fence at the end of the field.) I got in, turned on the switch, and pushed down on the foot-operated starter. When the engine turned over a few times and didn't start, I saw him reach over and pull out the throttle. Now that I think about it, since he couldn't see, he probably thought he was pulling out the choke. Anyway, the engine started and we were off like a shot. The cabbage was flying, we were heading straight for the fence, and I was frozen at the controls just trying to hang on. When we were about fifty feet from the fence, Granddad pushed the throttle in and we stopped. Though no damage was done, other than the cabbage, my uncles never let me forget about my trip through the cabbage patch.

One summer day, my family, my three cousins, they're parents, a girl, about our age, and her parents were visiting there on the farm. There was a horse drawn wagon setting near the barn. We decided we would get it started down the hill and take a little ride. We talked the girl into getting on, we got the wagon started and jumped on. As the wagon gained speed, we could see the situation was getting out of hand, so we bailed off and told the girl to get off too. She wouldn't budge. The wagon continued on down the hill picking up speed, running through a fence, tearing it down, and coming to a stop in a thicket at the bottom of the hill. Though she had a pretty wild ride, she came through it unscathed. Over the years, my cousins and I spent a lot of time in the barn jumping out of the loft in to hay on the bottom floor. Occasionally for a thrill or because of a dare, we would do a flip on the way down. If you landed properly, it was fine. If you landed on your head; later you had a sore neck. One day I was in the orchard wearing a pair of tennis shoes, tennis shoes of those days had a very thin sole. I saw some boards laying under a tree and stepped on them. As I did, I felt a very severe pain in my right foot. As I looked down, I saw a nail sticking up through my shoe. I didn't have to take my shoe off to know it had gone through my foot. Another episode involved the same foot. I was about eight years old. Early one morning while going bear footed, (no Hillbilly worth his salt would wear shoes in summer, especially on the farm.) I went out to the wood lot. Seeing an axe and a short piece of board there, I decided to split the board. I laid the board against a block of wood, put my right foot on the bottom to hold it and I swung the axe. The sharpened axe went through the entire length of the board and also through my right big toe. When I looked down, my toe made a perfect Y. This resulted in a trip to the doctor, my vacation being curtailed, and me walking on crutches for a while. When staying on the farm, after the work was done, one of our uncles would load us in the truck and take us to the swimming hole, a place called Fall Rock. This was about two miles down the hill below my granddad's farm. My mother went to the one room school that is still standing nearby.

My granddad grew all kinds of produce on the farm that he would take to Beckley, about twenty miles away, and sell to his regular customers. My cousin and I would go along, riding in the back of the truck with the produce. He also sold milk. One day while going up a steep hill, my cousin let a five gallon can of milk turn over spilling the milk. Afterwards, that hill was always referred to as Milk Hill.

The up stairs walls and ceilings were papered with newspapers instead of regular wallpaper. Wallpaper cost money my grandparents didn't have. I still remember lying in bed and reading the newspaper adds. A new Ford was priced at $883.00

When all of the family came to the farm for dinner, nobody before or since could fix a meal like my grandmother. We would eat at a long table on a screened in back porch. There would be two kinds of potatoes, two kinds of beans, two kinds of bread and etc. I would eat until I was in misery.

One winter day my cousin and I decided we would ride the school bus to the farm, spend the night, and ride the bus back to school the next morning. It seemed like a good idea that day, but the next morning there was a very deep snow, and it was drifting. My uncles took a team of horses out to the road and tried to break through the drifts, but even the horses couldn't get through. It sure tore us up to have to miss school and stay there and eat grandmother's good cooking, but somehow we survived.

The old two story house burned in the late forties or early fifties. It was replaced with a smaller house. Today it stands empty as my last living uncle passed away. The old barn, though showing it's age, is still there.

Coal Fields

A year later my dad went to work in the coalfields. He worked in the shop of the Lilly brook Coal Company. We later moved there in October 1933. We lived in this mining town of about 300 homes for about six years. In the fall of 1939, as the war expanded, my dad was called back to work by the railroad, and we moved back to Hinton. One memory I still have of Lillybrook occurred on July 9, 1936. A friend, Donald Stockman, had been at my house most of the day. Just before dark a large black cloud came over the top of the mountain. My mom told him he had better go home as it looked like a storm was coming. That night there was a very bad storm, resulting in a flood, in which both Donald and his mother were drowned. I also remember gathering empty coke bottles, 24 to the case for which we received 10 cents at the company store. Although I have a lot of memories of Lillybrook, some good some bad, I was still glad to move back to Hinton.

1940's

Though Hinton would probably be called "low-key" by the big city kids, my three cousins, who lived nearby, and myself seldom witnessed a dull moment. In the fall and winter we went hunting in the surrounding mountains. It was quite an experience to get up early and be in the woods before daylight, and then wait sitting under a big shaley bark hickory for the squirrels to move after daylight. Unless it was windy early in the morning, it was usually foggy during that time of year. It was also exciting to take a bead on a squirrel in top of those big hickories and watch them fall 30 to 40 feet to the ground. The gray squirrel of West Virginia presented much more of a challenge than the red squirrel of Indiana, where I now live. The local kids would also gather in winter on the nearby creek to ice skate or to sleigh ride down the hills in the area. Some of these rides were attempted by only the most adventurous.

Sandy

One day I got home from school, got my rifle, and headed for the creek. On warm days snakes would climb out on bushes above the creek to sun themselves, and I would shoot them out. We had a bulldog names Sandy, who always went with me. On this day however, when I got home Sandy wasn't around, so I thought I would sneak off without him just to see what his reaction would be. When I got to the creek, I crossed over to the other side and sat down on a big rock to watch for the snakes. The creek in this area had an uneven rock bottom that was very slick and covered with only about four inches of water. Soon I heard him coming through the field running as fast as he could. When he reached the water's edge, he didn't even slowdown. He hit the water at full speed. His feet started going in all directions on the slick rock. Just in front of him was a huge rock, and since he couldn't get stopped, he went head on into it. After the collision, he got back on his feet, shook his head, and took off for the house. I don't know if he thought I caused his problem, or if he thought it just wasn't his day. Nevertheless, he'd had enough.

The Mule Slide

In the summer, we were usually playing in the woods, riding wagons, (some of them including mine, home made) or skinny dipping in one of our favorite swimming holes in the creek. One swimming hole where we spent most of our time was called " The Mule Slide. " It consisted of a solid rock chute, approximately 50 to 60 feet long, with a surface as slick as glass. At the bottom of the chute was a large pool. The proper procedure was to run along the creek (no bathing suite), until reaching top speed at the top of the chute. At this time you would leap into the chute and travel at great speed until you went off into the pool below. To say the least, it was quite refreshing on a hot summer day.

Crazy

On other days we rode bicycles down hills or mountain roads at high speeds that might have been considered somewhat dangerous or downright ridiculous, considering it was in county rode and state road traffic. I guess the granddaddy of all bicycle runs for us was down Beech Run Mountain. This was a six mile curvy road from Nimitz to the bottom of the mountain. There is one curve on this mountain that was in Ripley's Believe It Or Not. There is a building in this curve, and as you go around the curve, you can see all four sides of the building. We would hitch a ride on a big truck, with our bikes, to the top of the mountain, and then ride back down. It was on this same curvy mountain road, in later years, we would race our Fords and Chevies on moon light nights from the bottom to the top. We would turn our headlights off in the curves to see if we were meeting a car. If not, we could use both sides of the road to make the curve. Looking back, this was one sport we had that I would not recommend to anyone.

Fear

I suppose there are some people who have never had an occasion to experience extreme fear, such as loss of life or serious injury. I have been in that position more than once in my lifetime. The first time was when I was about twelve years old. Probably the reason I was that scared was because I was so young. I would work with my dad on the farm in the morning. After lunch he would leave for work on the railroad. Before leaving he would tell me the work he wanted me to do in the afternoon. This particular afternoon he wanted me to cut the tops out of some tall trees on the hill in front of our house. One tree was a tall sycamore. I had to climb up the tree about forty feet from the ground. It was about another forty feet to the creek at the bottom of the hill below. Anytime you are looking down, it looks twice as far as when you are looking up. While hanging in that tree, the height alone scared me to death, but then I began to wonder, when I cut the top out of this tree and it begins to fall, will it pull the top of the tree over? Will I be able to hold on to the saw with one hand and the tree with the other? Will I wind up in the creek below? I never had a safety belt and I guess it never occurred to me to tie myself to the tree. Anyway, it all did work out. The top broke clean, I hung on to the saw, and I did hold on. Although that was sixty some years ago, it is still very clear in my mind.

One of my most vivid memories of living on the creek is the day I was shot on top of a mountain. A friend Robert Frazier, was with me along with another neighborhood friend, Benny Neely. It was Ben who pointed his empty (or at least he thought it was) rifle at me. He said "Bang" and the gun went off. I was the third kid in the neighborhood over a period of years to be shot accidentally. The first died instantly. The second one paralyzed from the waist down, lived approximately a year after being shot. After it happened, Ben started for the bottom of the mountain to call an ambulance. I remember I was sitting on the ground leaning against a fence at the time, and I kept trying to pass out. My vision kept narrowing down, and I kept shaking my head for I was afraid I wouldn't wake up. It finally narrowed down to just a very small opening, about the size of a baseball, and then it opened up to normal. Robert and I then started down the mountain. He would carry me as far as he could, which wasn't very far for we were about the same size, and then I would walk as far as I could with him holding on to me. We finally made it to the bottom of the mountain to my aunt's house where the ambulance was supposed to come to. Shortly thereafter (though it seemed like forever to me), the ambulance arrived, and we were on our way to the hospital. No one knows how good that hospital looked to me. The doctor said "The bullet had entered my chest, passed through my lungs, missing my heart by one half inch, and exited my back, missing my spine by one eight inch. When I left the hospital they said it would be six weeks before I could walk. Three days later while my parents were gone I tried to walk but it didn't work. Though I still beat the six-week schedule.

Another memory is of a bicycle ride. Again my friend, Robert, was with me. We were double heading on his bicycle down a long hill on a one lane, hard surfaced road. Just as we reached the bottom of the hill, we met a car and had to get off on the berm. I remember looking over Robert's shoulder and seeing a small mud puddle directly ahead of us. The berm was only about three feet wide and then it dropped off a rock wall about four feet to the creek. The next thing I remember seeing was the top of some bushes that I was flying over the top of, and then I remember nothing. I don't know how much later it was, but when I came to, Robert had carried me to another aunt's house about 200 yards away. We were down in the basement, and I was trying to get out the basement door. Robert was holding me and saying I couldn't go out. I asked," Why Not?" He said, "Your nose is broken, and all the skin is off the side of your face. Your mother is here, and she will see you." I said, "Robert, I don't care if she is here, I have to get to a doctor." I had landed face first in the rocky creek bed. Life was anything but low key for us kids.

  As we got older, we began to spend more time on the river fishing, swimming, and boating. As teenagers, one of our favorite swimming places was in the river near the Moose club just east of town. There was a cable hanging from a tall tree on the river's edge, and we could swing on it out over the river and drop off. There was a rock ledge that extended out a ways from the bank. You had to be sure you cleared the ledge before you dropped off the cable. One day while we were swimming there, a schoolmate came to join us. Since this was his first time to swim there, we told him not to let go of the cable too soon, should he decide to swing on it. Shortly thereafter, he did swing out on it. I saw him let go and dive for the water. It looked like he had let go a little too soon, and when he didn't surface right a way, we became concerned and started swimming toward him. However, before we reached him his head came up out of the water. It wasn't a pretty sight. He had struck the reef and his scalp was hanging down in front of his face. He was taken to the hospital and later released.

  Soon I was in high school and the pace seemed to quicken. I got a job at a theater in town where I worked after school and on weekends taking up tickets. Although the pay wasn't good, by any standards, I did get to see all the movies free.

  As soon as I was sixteen, I got my driver's license and started driving a dry cleaning and laundry truck in the evening after school and on Saturday. On the weekends I would go to the local airport and spend my paycheck for the week taking flying lessons. This airport was called the Nimitz Airport and was located on top of a mountain. The morning I took my solo flight, the sun was shinning brightly, so I took off into a clear blue sky. My logbook says that was September 8, 1945. I was really enjoying this ride and everything was going well until about thirty minutes later, when I returned to the airport to land. In the half hour I had been gone, the fog had risen off the river and completely covered the airport that I was looking for. Just the fact that this was my first trip alone had me a little edgy, but now what? Looking at the gas gauge I saw I still had plenty of fuel left, and I knew I was in the general area of the airport, so I decided to just sit up there and do doughnuts until the situation improved. A short time late, a hole opened up in the fog, and I went down through it to find the airport was still there.

  After I had gotten enough experience that I was confident about flying (my parents still didn't know I was taking flying lessons). I flew down the valley, where we lived and circled over the house. When I came home that evening, my mom knowing my interest in airplanes said, "Jack, there was a plane flying over the house today, and I have never seen one that low." I still didn't tell her it was me.

Driving The Truck

Driving the dry cleaning truck had its advantages. This was during the war, when tires couldn't be bought, and you had to have ration stamps to buy gasoline. I was given a stamp by my employer to buy four gallons of gas per day for the truck. I soon learned that by coasting down all of the hills I could save a stamp approximately every other day. Though I didn't have a car, my friends did, and we always had stamps for gas.

One summer afternoon I had completed my dry cleaning route early. I happened to meet up with a few friends and we decided to take the truck and visit a couple of schoolmates who lived several miles away in a small community called Jumping Branch. Later that afternoon after letting my friends out, I reported in to the dry cleaner's office. Just as I walked in, the phone rang. Since I was the closest to it, I answered it. The lady on the phone said, "I have some cleaning I would like for you to pick up." I said "Fine, where do you live?" She said, "On route 3 at Jumping Branch." I replied, "Lady, we do not have a route out that way." She said, "Yes you do. I just saw one of your trucks out here." With the boss being there in the office this conversation became rather difficult. I was trying to get this woman off my back, and at the same time not saying anything that would tip the boss off as to where I had been. I finally got through this ordeal with out letting the cat out of the bag, but I never took the truck to Jumping Branch again.

As I was going through high school my dad said more than once, "Jack, as soon as you are out of school, you should go to the railroad and put in your application for an electrician apprentice ship. I always said, "ok", but really working in the shops never seemed to be my thing. The day I told him I was leaving for the service, he said, " be sure to get your electrician application in before you leave." I stopped in the railroad office, but the clerk I had to see was out of the office at the time. Since I was leaving the next day, I wasn't about to spend my time waiting for him.

While I was going to high school, there was a C&O Engineer, Mr. Beasley, who lived in the neighborhood. Sometimes before the school bus came, Mr. Beasley would offer us a ride to school, if he were going that way. During the ride with him one day, I remember him telling us how he liked his job, and if we were going to work for the railroad, we should hire out in engine service. After going in service, I never saw Mr. Beasley again, but I never forgot what he said.

During our junior year of high school, my cousin's dad bought a 1937 Ford, black tudoor sedan from a farmer. This cousin's name was Charles, but we called him Todd. Though this car was six years old, it looked like a new. It had low mileage because it had been in storage for years. Todd was permitted to use the car under one condition that we didn't go out of town. That went well for a while, but on one cold winter night, we decided we wanted to see what the action would be like in Beckley. Beckley was only twenty miles away, and we would be back by midnight. There were three of us in the car: Todd, Robert Frazier, and myself. Later that night in Beckley, it started to rain and then to freeze. We decided to head back for Hinton. Although it was only twenty miles, there were three mountains to cross; Big White Oak, Little White Oak and Beech Run. Even before we got out of Beckley the streets were a sheet of ice and the rain was changing to snow. We made it down Raleigh hill and through Cherry Tree Dip; How ever as we topped Glade Creek Hill, we could see lights everywhere. We soon realized they were cars setting at all angles, stuck on the hill. Our first reaction was to stop, but with the snow on top of the ice, it seemed as though, we just went faster. Setting first out in the middle of the road was a 1941 Plymouth and we hit it head on. Thereby changing the history of both that car and my uncle's Ford. At the time of the impact, I heard someone scream and thought someone was seriously injured. Later we learned, when we hit the Plymouth it went back into a Model A Ford setting behind it. The Model A was a four door and a woman had the back door open and was standing behind it. The door had hit her and knocked her in the side ditch. Only her dignity was hurt. The man driving the Plymouth was a little bit intoxicated. Since his car would still run he asked if we would help him get his car to the top of the hill to which we agreed. When we were almost to the top of the hill, he began to talk about a lawsuit for damages, so we told him to get up the hill the best way he could. He immediately had a change of heart and said to forget the suit and just get him up the hill. Of course, during the war auto parts were hard to come by, so my uncle's ford never looked the same again, and our privileges with the car were severely curtailed.

Outhouse
When it did get boring in "River City," we usually found a way to pick up the pace, as we did one Halloween night. We took an outhouse out in the country and brought it in town on a pick up truck. Around midnight, at the main intersection of town, we took the street name off the pole on the corner. While we had lookouts posted for the cops, we lifted the outhouse up and set it down over the street sign pole so it couldn't be moved. The next morning it was still there, and the street department had to be called out to remove it. There was a nice write up in the paper the next day, but they never found out who did it.

Military Service
In September 1946, I enlisted for eighteen months in the army and left for Fort Hayes in Columbus, Ohio to be inducted. From there we went to Camp Attabury, Indiana and then to Fort Knox, Kentucky for six weeks basic training. After four weeks, we were given week- end passes but were told not to leave the area. As soon as I got off the fort, I was on a bus to West Virginia. I got back to base Sunday night and no one was the wiser. Two weeks later we finished basic training and were given orders to ship out to California for the Far East. Some of my training companions went to Japan and others to

Korea and was given five days travel time with nine days delay in route. When my former boss heard I was home, he called and said, "Jack, you have got to help me out a few days because I am short on drivers." Since he had always been good to me, I finally agreed to work two or three days to help him out.

On the day I was supposed to catch the train to California, I didn't. Though I don't remember the particulars for not leaving that day, I'm sure it must have been pretty important at the time. The following day, I caught a train for Chicago and it got there too late to make the connection with the troop train leaving for California that day. Therefore I had another fourteen-hour delay. When we reached Camp Stoneman, California, the officer in charge said, " You who are on time, good-you who are late, shame on you." Shortly after we arrived, it started raining, and it rained continuously for three days. I know for we sat outside on benches in it day and night. Meanwhile they keep processing men around us. We later found out the building at Fort Knox containing our records had burned, thus causing the delay. Also since they didn't have a record of our shots now, they were giving us all of them over. As we went in the building where they were giving the shots, they were putting a stamp on the guys who had to take all of the shots over I knew I had received all my shots before, so when they put the stamp on my arm, I spit on my hand, rubbed the stamp off and passed on through.

The following day, we boarded the troop ship Gordon Mc Cray while a band played "Sentimental Journey". Just before dark, we passed under the Golden Gate. Soon the front and rear of the ship began to move up and down. As we got farther out to sea, it also began to roll from side to side. It was then I began to feel a little uncomfortable, and I continued to feel that way for a couple of days, though I never really got sick. The guy in the bunk above me never got out of his bunk the whole trip of approximately thirty days except to go to the bathroom. During this time all he ate was candy bars. We went through some pretty bad storms. During one of them, one of the guys I had gone through basic training with was thrown against a bulkhead and killed. They put him in the deep freeze until we got to Japan. There were others who received serious injuries. We had to stand at long tables to eat. As the ship would roll, the hot coffee that was in metal pitchers would slide back and forth. We could usually control them, but if it got too out of hand everyone ran, and the coffee went everywhere. There was no hot water for the showers, just ocean water. In December, that took some getting use to.

We landed in Yokohama, Japan on December 24,1946. The next morning we had chip beef on toast for breakfast. Never having eaten this before, I thought it was Japanese food.

Someone didn't have his or her act together or else we were ripped off by the black market. The first thirty days, other than breakfast, the food was lousy. About all we had was fish and stew. After that, however, the food did get better. I remember looking at a can of chicken we were having for dinner in December, 1946, and it had been canned in 1942.

On January 16, one of the guys got scarlet fever, so we were all put on quarantine. We were released on the 24th and on the 26th, then the guy in the bunk above me was diagnosed with it, and we were all quarantined again.

On the following day we were moved to Fuchu Racetrack, approximately 30 miles or so from Tokyo, where we were to remain in quarantine. By this time I had been transferred from F troop to E troop. I thought the food would be better, but I found little difference. In September 1947, our company was awakened at 3:15 am and left around 4:00 am for the train station. By train, we traveled into the mountain country where we made camp at the base of Mt Fugiama. We were on maneuvers for practically a month and were sleeping in tents. We had two blankets each, but due to being in high elevation, it got very cold at night. With nothing under you, except the canvas of the cot, two blankets were not enough to keep warm. Above us was Mt Fugi and below was a huge lake. From the high elevation, at times we could look down on top of the clouds floating above the lake. After completing both day and night maneuvers we moved back to our quarters at Fuchu. On October 13th, we returned to our regiment in Tokyo. Later that same month we were assigned to guard towers on the docks of Tokyo Bay. This wasn't bad duty at first as we were on duty four hours and off eight. We also got to watch the ship traffic come and go which was rather interesting. However, when cold weather came, it got down right uncomfortable. On December 1st, I got notice giving me a choice of signing up for two more years or going home two months early. My question was, where do I get my boat ticket? On December 4th, I went on duty from 4:00 to 8:00 am and was relieved from duty to await shipping orders home.

On December 11th, at 3:30 pm, we boarded the ship General Hodges, though we didn't cast off until 2:35 pm, on the 12th. The trip was much smoother coming back. No big storms like we had going over. On December 23rd, at 3:30 am, we came in sight of the lighthouse, cut the ship's engines, and lay outside of Frisco Bay until daylight. Just after sun up, we passed under the Golden Gate Bridge.

Before I left for service, I had lived on a farm, but I didn't drink milk. After I left the states on my way to Japan, I never saw fresh milk until I returned to Frisco. Fresh milk, a chocolate shake, and a grilled ham sandwich were what I wanted more than anything else. My first night in Frisco I had all three. On January 3rd, I got my discharge, said goodbye to my buddies, and boarded a DC3 out of Oakland, Cal to Chicago.

While I was in service I wanted to get some kind of training I could use in civilian life, but that never seemed to materialize. Due to my shooting experience before entering the service, I was a pretty good shot, which showed up on my records at the firing range. Thus the army wanted me to be a machine gunner, and they usually have their way. I did travel a lot and saw a lot of sights I otherwise would not have seen. They paid me every month and gave me the G I Bill that paid for three and a half years of my four-year college education later on. I was given an opportunity to go to Officer's Candidate School, but in order to do so, I would have to sign up for two more years, and I did not want to do that. I made a lot of friends, some of whom I still keep in touch with. So I guess it wasn't too bad. It might have been better, but I'm sure it could have been worse.

I left California in the warm sunlight, never expecting the blowing snowstorm that waited when we landed in Chicago. The temperature was about 30 degrees, the snow was about a foot deep with a 30 mph wind, and I was in my summer khakis. I had decided rather than go directly to West Virginia; I would stop in Peru, Indiana to see my sister and brother-in-law.

At 7:00 pm, I caught a bus for Indiana, arriving January 5, 1948. My brother-in-law, Staten Morris, was a dispatcher for the Chesapeake & Ohio Railroad in Peru. He had formerly transferred from the Huntington Division in WVa. He told me the railroad was hiring a lot of men: brakeman, switchman, telegraph operators and fireman. Brakemen was promoted to conductors; telegraph operators to dispatchers (dispatchers put out orders and control the switches trains operate by) and fireman were promoted to engineers. He told me I could probably have my choice, if I wanted to hire out. I decided I wanted to go back to West Virginia for a while and think it over. The next day I took a train out of Peru for Cincinnati where I caught the C&O's passenger, The George Washington. In it's hey day it was the C&O's best. The passenger cars had aquariums, magazine racks, hostesses, movies and fantastic dining cars. Leaving Cincinnati at 7:00 pm, I was unable to see all the beautiful scenery while passing through the New River Gorge. They have since changed the schedule so Amtrak now goes through in the daytime. Having traveled this route many times in years gone by, I knew, by the station names the conductor was calling, when we were getting close to my hometown. Finally the conductor came through and said, "Hinton, coming in sight." We arrived at 12:52 am on January 7, 1948. The first person I saw on the platform was my Uncle Roy Dobbins, the one who owned the car my cousin and I had wrecked about a year before I had left for service. I guess he had forgiven us for he seemed happy to see me.

Working For Dravo

After I was home a few days, my dad, who was shop foreman in charge of locomotive repairs, insisted that I put in my application for apprentice at the C&O shop. A few days later I found myself at the clerk's office at the railroad. She said they were not hiring, but she would take my application and put me at the bottom of the list. When she looked on the application and saw my name was Jack Young, she asked if I knew Charlie young? I said, "Yes, he is my dad." She said, "Well then, we will put you at the top of the list." I told her no, I didn't want any favors. Really, I was just trying to please my dad for working in the shops just didn't seem to be my cup of tea.

Some of the local guys, who had been in service with me, decided to go to Concord College, located about 30 miles away, and they enrolled for the fall semester. I went along to look around, and though I wanted to use my G I Bill, I didn't feel I was ready just yet.

At this time, Dravo Corporation was building a flood control dam on New River in Hinton. I had a friend working in the office there who suggested I apply for a job. Though I hadn't forgotten what Mr. Beasley had said about an engineer's job being a good one, I still wasn't sure if I wanted to leave West Virginia and my relatives and friends that I had grown up with there. I knew it would be a lifetime commitment for when you establish seniority on a division; you could not transfer to another division. I had a cousin working as a fireman out of Hinton. He suggested I hire out there, but I remembered engineers being cut off on that division for years at a time. I also knew I would move up much faster on the Chicago Division because there were a lot of older engineers working there. I decided to go to work for Dravo and take a little more time to think about going to Indiana.

When I went to work for Dravo, they had been working on the dam since before I left for military service, so it was now approximately one hundred feet in the air. At first it was a little scary but soon the height was no problem. No one was killed while I worked there due to accidents. However, a scaffold rope broke one day and five workers slid approximately seventy-five feet down a trash chute. They were all hospitalized as they had lost a lot of skin in the slide. One of my duties as a carpenter helper was to take the handsaws to the file shop, located near the base of the dam, to be sharpened. At this day in time, there was no such thing as a skill saw. In order to get to the file shop, I had to walk down a long set of steps and back up these same steps on the return trip. Several weeks later while returning from the file shop carrying two saws; I noticed a ladder going straight up the face of the dam. I could see this would be quite a short cut as compared to walking over to and then up the steps. When I had climbed up the ladder approximately forty feet, I suddenly felt the ladder give a lurch. I knew there was not anything above me, so I quickly looked below. What I saw gave me a chill. One of the four big cranes located on top of the dam was hooked to a huge I beam. The beam was approximately fifty feet long, three to four feet high, and nearly three feet wide. I had no idea what that beam would weigh, but I knew the crane was lifting the beam, and one end of the beam was dragging on the ladder. I also knew if the beam would snag on the ladder, it would jerk it off the dam, and I would be history. I went up the rest of that ladder like a shot never again to take that short cut.

I liked the job pretty well. The work was outside, the pay was good, and I was staying at home. A few months later I realized when this job was finished, I would have to leave town or possibly the state to remain in this kind of work with this company and I would be forever moving from one location to another. Also on rainy days, we couldn't work and that reduced our pay considerably. With this thought in mind, I boarded the C&O passenger out of Hinton for Indiana. I put my application in for a position as locomotive fireman on June 21, 1948. I passed my company physical on June 23rd, and was approved for employment on July 15th. I was hired by C.T. Markley Road Foreman Of Engines and was called to take my first student trip shortly thereafter. These trips consisted of one trip out of the terminal each way East to Cincinnati approximately 156 miles and West to Chicago 117 miles. Also we had to spend one day on a yard job. These jobs made up trains or switched cars in the yard at Peru. I tried to get my trips in as soon as possible for not only was they're no pay for these trips, but your seniority would not start until you had made a pay trip. The purpose of these student trips was to familiarize the student with the tools and machinery he would be using, as well as learning the geography of the railroad over which he would be operating. I was called for my first pay trip on July 27, 1948 and this established my seniority as of that date. This is an important date to a railroader because it will determine which jobs he will be able to hold out of Peru or away from home on an out post job. It also determined how much my income would be for no two jobs paid the same.

At this time the C&O's power consisted of steam engines only, except for a few Budd Cars (electric) out on the East Coast. On the Chicago Division, we used K-2's, and K-3's for main line service. Officially, these engines were called Mikado's. We called them

Mikes. Very few steam engines could compare to the Mikes in looks. They were good looking engines and good performers. The K-2's on the Chicago Division were numbered from 1160 through 1209. The K-3's were from 1210 to 1259. The K-2's engine and tender weight was 577,1000 pounds. The boiler pressure was 200 pounds, and cylinder horsepower was 2,824. The total engine length was approximately 50 feet. The tender's coal capacity was 15 tons and it held 12000gallons of water. These K-2's were built in 1924.

The K-3's total weight was 731,340 pounds. The boiler pressure was 200 pounds, horsepower was 2,824, coaltender capacity was 25 tons and held 21,000 gallons of water. Sometime back, my time books (these were books all train and engine crew members kept their time in, which included engine numbers, time and place of starting to work and where and when relieved) for 1948, 1949 and 1950 became misplaced. So I do not know exact days I worked on these engines but some of the engines we worked on in this time period were 1162, 1165, 1193, 1202, and 1177. The 1177 had been wrecked three times and several of the men did not like to work on it. They thought it was jinxed. We also had smaller steamers that were used to double head trains up the hill out of Peru. These engines were also used as yard engines. These were the G-7 class (G-280). This meant they had small pony trucks leading, four sets of drivers, and no small trailing pony trucks. Their numbers were in the 900 series. One we had was the 990. When these engines were used to double head up the hill out of Peru, they were called "Helper Engines)." They would be placed on the head end of a K-2 or K-3 and when topping Hoover's Hill at Twelve Mile, Indiana, they would be cut off and returned to Peru. Depending on the number of trains ran, a helper crew would help one to three trains up the hill in an eight-hour shift. I always preferred helper service to yard work, as the time seems to go much faster. The small helper engines were all hand fired. This meant the fireman shoveled the coal out of the tender into the fore box. Though it looked simple, there was an art to hand firing a steam engine. For best results, you had to keep a heal around the back of the fire box while keeping the fire light in the front of the fire box. The Mikes were stoker fired. They had an augur that ran from the tender to the firebox. By manipulating steam valves, at his seat, the fireman could regulate the amount of coal going to the firebox from the tender. There were times the stokers would malfunction and the engine would have to be hand fired to the next terminal. When you had to hand fire one of these big engines, you really earned your money. Speaking of money, the railroad was rather unique. The first day you made a pay trip, you earned the same amount as a fireman who had been working for five or ten years.

On July 27, 1948, the day of my first pay trip, I was excited to say the least. My brother-in-law gave me a ride to the caller's office where the engine crews reported for duty. Crews were called an hour in advance of reporting time. Calling time differed on different railroads from one to two hours. When I walked into the office, I saw what was called "the board". This board was about four feet wide, had a glass front and behind the glass was listed each job that worked out of Peru. There were assigned jobs, which were usually the most preferred jobs. These runs consisted of produce, meat, autos, auto parts, heavy machinery, appliances, lumber or other high revenue freight. On these jobs the crews knew what days they would be called to work and their calling times were fairly constant. Also on the assigned jobs you would have the same crew members with you each trip unless one laid off. If so, he would be relieved for that trip,

K 2 # 1174 eastbound out of Peru, Indiana

J.O. Young during steam engine days.

A K-2 leaving Peru west bound with a coal train.

K-2s double heading stopped for water.

Double Header with helper Engine on head end-
Westbound out of Peru, Indiana.

K 2 # 1170 westbound into Peru, Indiana

by a man off the extra board each of the assigned jobs on the Wabash Division, Peru to Chicago had two crews. Both the Wabash and the Miami Divisions had pool crews. These jobs worked first in first out. These jobs were paid by mileage and the number of crews in the pool was determined by the mileage the pool crews had run in the previous fifteen days. On pool jobs you had also the same crewmembers, unless someone lay off to be replaced by an extra man, but you did not know what day your job would be going out or coming in, in advance as you did on the assigned jobs. If at the check of the board, another crew were added to the pool, it would be placed at the bottom of the board, and as the crews were called out, would work its way up to first out. After being in the pool for awhile, you would pretty well know, from past experience, and information you could get, by calling the crew caller, the number of crews they plan to run out of the pool for the day. When you were first out, you had to stay near the phone or let the caller know at what phone you could be reached. If you missed a call, a man from the extra board would replace you.

Some of the older men preferred yard job. On these jobs you did not have to be away from home, if you had enough seniority to hold the yard jobs in the town where you lived. These jobs worked seven days a week, later five days, and were paid by the hour. We also had yard and transfer jobs away from home. Some of these were approximately sixty- five miles, some 117 miles, and some 156 miles. The youngest firemen and engineers usually worked these jobs.

Transfer jobs differed from yard jobs, as they left the yard to make pickups and deliveries to interchange points or to other railroads. Transfer jobs were paid on the hourly rate also.

Extra boards were usually held by the youngest men, or men who had turned down promotion. They were not permitted to hold regular jobs other than yard jobs or transfer jobs. On the extra board, you were called to fill any vacancy on the assigned jobs, pool jobs, yard jobs, wreck trains, or work trains. Also for messenger service (riding dead engines that were being moved between terminals.

Although I do not remember what my first trip was, I do remember it was called around 8:00 am and was coming back into Peru that day, so it was probably a work train doing some type of track or right of way work. A few days later I was called for a work train that would go to Cincinnati. About twenty miles west of Cincinnati we had to go into a side- track to meet a west bound. After waiting for quite sometime, I decided to get off the engine and stretch my legs. While doing so, I stepped on a nail near the engine and ran it through my shoe and foot. I had to be taken to a doctor in a nearby town and our train was delayed until I could return. This would be one of only two injuries I would receive in my forty years of railroading though I was involved in many crossing collisions and near misses later on during my years of service.

Before I hired out on the railroad, Staten my brother in law said there would come a time when as a young man in seniority, I would have to go out of town to work out post jobs. In just a few weeks this became a reality. I was called to work a job at Stoney Island. This was a terminal located on Stoney Island Avenue on the south side of Chicago. Having talked to some of the other railroad men, I never expected to find much there, but this place was really the pits. The Men on yard and transfer jobs stayed in a boxcar that had been converted into a camp car. It contained bunks for about six men, a rest room, shower and cooking facilities (ah la 1920's.) The men coming on road jobs stayed at a combined restaurant and rooming house we called "Old Lady Warrens.' The food was terrible and there was no air conditioning or screens on the windows for that matter. When one crew was called, the next crew- members would use the same beds without the linens being changed. On my following trips to Old Lady Warrens, I carried my own linens with me. Of all places I stayed while working on the railroad, this had to be the worst. On my first job at Stoney Island, we went to work at 3:59 P.M. We would get our engine from the ready track, go pick up our cars and caboose, and then go downtown Chicago to the stockyards. There we would spot cars for loading and then go eat or whatever for about an hour and a half while the cars were being loaded. We would then return, couple up the cars and deliver them back to the yard where they would be put on hot eastbound manifest trains. At least, that was how it was supposed to work. However, on my first day on the job, when I reported for work, I could tell the engineer had had a few drinks. When we returned from our break to couple our train, he was in no condition to run the train. Since the brakeman had been on the job longer than I had, he said he would try to run the engine. Though it was somewhat of a miracle, we did find our way back to south Chicago, arriving two hours late. The engineer on this job (I will call him Joe) remained with the company until his retirement. Though he was a good engineer when sober, he had and continued to have an alcohol problem. The company officials, though they suspected it, were never successful in catching him in the act. Many stories were told about Joe over the years. I was called to work as his fireman on an eastbound freight a few years later. At this time we were running F-7 diesel engines, and they were equipped with alarm bells to let the crew know when there was a malfunction in one of the units. As Joe and I sit in the cab waiting for a signal to leave the yard, I heard, or thought I heard, an alarm bell go off. I got up and started back to check on the units. Joe said, "Wait, that's my watch." He reached in his bag and pulled out a big alarm clock. Undoubtedly, his railroad watch was in a pawnshop somewhere until payday. At this time, the railroad paid on the 15th and 30th of the month and at times some of the men did run short on money during the fifteen day period. One day we were switching cars in the railroad yard at Chicago and we had a tank car loaded with wine next to the engine. One of the switchmen came up on the engine and told us this wine car was leaking. Since wine was Joe's favorite drink, he said, "Quick, go find a jug and let's catch some of that." A brakeman told me this story on Joe. They were stopped directly behind another train one night and as Joe had been in the bottle before coming to work, it wasn't long before he dozed off. One of the crewmembers, seeing he was asleep, decided to have some fun. He jumped up and yelled Joe, they're into us." Just from reflex, Joe grabbed the brake valve and put the brakes into emergency on the train. After Joe retired, he was walking home from a tavern along the railroad track when he was struck and killed by a train. There were many railroads in Chicago at this time, and the rail traffic was heavy. When catching these out post jobs off the extraboard, you had to remain there until relieved by the regular man on the job, or for fifteen days to be relieved by another man off the extra board. When relieved, you would catch a train to Peru and mark back up on the extra board. In those days we did our "Deadheading" (traveling on the train to and from outlying points, while not being a member of the crew of the train on which you were riding.) During steam engine days I always rode the caboose and I have a lot of good memories from trips taken on a caboose. In those days they were equipped with a pot bellied, coal fired stove. These stoves were used for heat and to cook on. Some of the train crews slept on the cabooses, as they were equipped with bunks. After the train crew left the terminal the conductor and the flagman would ride in the cupola where they could watch the train from the rear for hot boxes (overheated wheel bearings), other mechanical problems, or for someone trying to break in the cars while the train was stopped. If it were at night, I would usually sleep on a bunk or read by one of the coal oil lamps. In later years, the cabooses were equipped with generators, electric lights and fuel oil stoves. There was usually a hot pot of coffee on the stove, while in route, and sometimes we would share a hot meal with the crew. Sometimes the caboose was full of guys from one or two crews that were deadheading from terminal to terminal. This would happen when there was more business in one direction, thus the unneeded crews would be deadheaded back to their home terminal. On these occasions it was party time, story telling, playing cards and so fourth. Though deadheading crews were being paid, there wasn't any work for them, except in emergency situations. On cold winter nights, it was quite relaxing to lay on a caboose cot, feel the heat from the old potbellied stove in the dim light of the coal oil lamp, and listen to the clickity clack of the wheels hitting rail joints as we headed home.

It was good to get back to Peru and the big stoker fired "Mikes", on the road jobs, instead of the hand fired yard and transfer jobs in Chicago. I would still catch a yard job off the extraboard now and then but at least not every day.

When I first came to Peru I stayed with my sister and brother –in-law until due to a family increase, they needed my bedroom. I then got a room in a private home where I also ate when I was there at mealtime.

The Chicago Division I worked on out of Peru was a single tracked road. It had numerous sidetracks where trains could meet or pass. At this time, operators located in towers, depots, or cabins along the tracks, controlled the signals. The operators got their instructions from dispatchers in Peru over company phone and telegraph lines. In the months to come I would have a lot to learn working outpost, yard and transfer jobs that I would catch off the extraboard, or when I was forced off the extraboard due to a slack in business. Also there was the geography of the road, location of the signals, meanings of the signals, location of the switches and derails that were located along the line to be learned. Most important thing for me at the time being was learning to fire the big road engines. Though they were stoker fired, there was an art to operating the stokers and blowers. (Blowers increased the draft in the firebox for faster combustion and helped to eliminate black smoke from the stack, while the stokers were delivering a load of coal to the firebox.) There were two stokers on each engine. One was located on each side of the firebox. Valves located in front of the fireman operated both stokers.

Working off the extraboard, you seldom had the same engineer twice in a row. All the engineers ran their engines differently, and the fireman had to fire his engine according to how that particular engineer operated. The engineer wanted the steam pressure held as close as possible to the maximum operating pressure, without going over it for that would set off the blow off cock. This would cause a loss of steam and water, and in turn the engineer might have to make an extra water stop. This would increase his running time for the trip, and possibly cause him to be run around by another train. - Perfect setting for an angry engineer. Some engineers were easier to fire for than others. The engineer regulated the amount of water going into the boiler, and he also determined the amount of water carried in the boiler. Some engineers carried more water than others in the boiler and this made it harder to fire the engine. There were three seats on the engine: one for the engineer, one for the brakeman, and one for the fireman. There was also a cushioned lid on the icebox where we carried our drinking water that could be used for an extra seat if necessary. There was a canvas curtain across the back of the cab that could be closed in cold weather. The steam engines had a smell all of there own. An odor made up of a mixture of coal smoke, warm oil, grease, hot steam pipes and the steam it's self. Not a bad odor, not a good odor, just a different odor. Anytime one of the crew ate an orange, he would put the pealing on the hot boiler head and that would make a pleasant odor in the cab. The steamers were different from the diesels as there was not a steady sound coming from the engine when sitting still. Occasionally you would hear the air pumps make their own unique sound. No sound thrilled the crews of steamers, on the Chicago Division, as coming up Okeann Hill through the Bluestone Cut with a tonnage train. (A tonnage train was a train that had the maximum tonnage the engine pulling that train was rated for.) At this time, the engines would be down to a very slow speed and pulling very hard. The crews said, "The engines were barking."

When hired, I was given a time card which listed stations, time schedules of assigned runs, track speeds, permanent slow orders, such as speeds through towns, around curves and etc. A rulebook that listed company rules, a book on the operating rules would be learned as soon as possible by study and observing on the job. The parts and operation of the steam engine were a little more involved so to learn this; you were given a little more time. However, when time for promotion came for engineer, you were expected to pass a written test on this material, along with a test on air brakes, operating rules and signals. Fireman were usually promoted to engineers no sooner than three to four years at the earliest, depending on the need for engineers at the time. At this time there was no age limit for retirement, so some of them worked as long as they could pass the physical and climb up into the cab.

I soon found out that automobiles, trucks and locomotives had a way of getting together on the crossings, and though my first experience with this was not serious, it was an indication of things to come. On this particular trip we were westbound out of Cincinnati and had stopped at Marion, Indiana. While sitting there, probably waiting for orders, someone had parked a car upon the hill above the track and left it. Evidently, the brake had not been set. It came down the hill and ran into the side of the locomotive. Though there was no damage to the locomotive, the Chevy did not fair so well.

It was some time later, after I had several road trips, my railroading career almost came to an end. I was called to fire an eastbound pool job to Cheviot, Ohio. This was our terminal at the east end of our division, located about six miles west of Cincinnati. We were on the westbound trip to Peru. I was leaning out the window looking down the track through the side window, when the engineer said something to me. I didn't hear what he said, so I pulled my head inside and asked him what he had said. At that same time there was a very loud noise on my side of the engine. When I looked around, the side window I had been looking through was gone. The engineer stopped the train immediately, and we found an eccentric rod, approximately four foot long, had come off and was thrown along my side of the cab shearing off the side window that I had been behind just a few seconds before.

Along about this time I was cut off, so I returned to West Virginia while waiting to be called back. One slow sunny afternoon, seven of us guys were sitting in Harper's Dairy Bar trying to think of some way to liven things up. Soon we were in a game of follow the leader with seven automobiles. I was driving my dad's car. After this became boring, we decided to stage a car wreck. We drove one car up a bank against a utility pole, raised the hood and pulled off a few hubcaps. Then I backed my dad's car up behind it and pulled away, spinning the tires, so it would look like the car slide up against the pole. Now it looked like the real thing. On Sunday afternoon, everyone went for an afternoon drive. Well they all went that day and it seemed they all came to see the wreck because the traffic was really backing up on this two- lane highway. It was at this time, I spotted a State Police car back in the stopped line of traffic. We tried to straighten up this very realistic looking mishap but were not able to do so before the policeman was on the scene asking if anyone was hurt. We said no, and he ask who was driving the wrecked car? One of my friends, we called "Buggs", told him it was he and he ask to see his license. I said, "Officer, this was not a wreck, we just drove the car up against the pole." He said, "Yes, I can see that by the skid marks." I told him I had made the skid marks with another car. He said, "Let me see your license also." He later let me go, but since Buggs gave him some lip about what the charge would be, he gave him a ticket.

If you were called for an outpost job at Muncie or Richmond and you had to be there for more than one day, you had to find your own place to stay. At Cheviot, as in Chicago, we stayed in a company rooming house that had a restaurant. Though the place we stayed in at Cheviot was not as bad as Old Lady Warrens in Chicago, it still left a lot to be desired. It was called "The Dog." That in it's self might give some indication of what it was like. It was a large two-story building with a front porch where the crewmembers would spend a lot of time in good weather. The ones that couldn't find a seat would sit on the steps or the porch railing. There was probably about as much railroading went on there as out on the main line, for you never got railroaders together that they didn't have lots of stories to tell about happenings of recent trips. While pilots call it "Hanger Flying" railroaders call it "making the cinders fly." From the front porch you went into the restaurant area. There was a long marble counter with bar stools and there were also booths along the facing wall. When the weather was too bad for the front porch, this was where the cinders flew. To the left, as you entered, was a small room that was used as a card room. Beyond this room was a large room with five or six beds. The north side of this room was adjacent to an unpaved alleyway that led to a ready mix plant. If you had to sleep during the day and this was the only room you could get, Lord help you, for there would be no sleep. In summer, with no air conditioning, the windows had to be kept open. With crews coming and going, and the trucks going every few minutes, you might as well have saved the fifty cents you paid for the bed. Up stairs there were some separate rooms and some that were portioned off like stalls. As these rooms were at least warm in the winter, they were the most desired. Sometimes you had to wait for a crew to be called before you could get a bed. At the back, on the bottom floor, was a barracks type room with cots. We called this room the "Bull Pin." In winter, it was like sleeping in a corncrib.

Though the food was much better here at the "Dog," than where we stayed in Chicago, I guarantee that no worse tasting coffee was ever made than what we had here. After I was married, I told my wife how bad it was many times, but she said, " Oh, it couldn't be that bad." One trip I left some in my thermos bottle and when I got home, I offered her a drink As soon as she tasted it, she blew it out. Luckily she was standing in front of the kitchen sink. I know it wasn't the coffee they were using, for many times I watched them put in the coffee, and they were using Maxwell House. I think it had something to do with not cleaning the pot.

At this time they were running turns out of Cheviot to Losantville. On the turns they would put an extra engine on the head end to help pull up the hills between Cheviot and Losantville. From here, one engine could handle the train on the more level track to Peru. At Losantville, just east of Muncie, was a Y track where the extra engine could be turned and run light back to Cheviot. When you left Peru on a pool job east, you never knew for sure when you would be back. On a normal trip you would only be gone two days, but if you caught two or three turns, you might be gone a week. Sometimes, though you had been called to double head to Losantville, when you arrived there you would get a message saying double head through to Peru. This could have been from needing the engine, or engine crew, in Peru. Nevertheless, it was always a welcome instruction. On one of these trips, I was called out of Cheviot on a double header for Peru. The engineer I was with, as well as the engineer on the other engine, were both very young engineers. It seemed they wanted to see how fast they could make that train run. Though we did make it to Peru, through some of the curves, I wasn't sure we would.

As I worked and tried to learn as much as I could in the coming trips, I found most all of the guys great to work with, however, since there wasn't any forced retirement, we had a couple of "old goats" I would soon get to know. I was called out of Chicago one night on a hot manifest. When we stopped for coal and water at English Lake, as the engineer was getting off the engine to oil around, he told me to shake the grates. I went back to take coal and water and then got back on the engine and shook the grates. When he came back up on the engine the first thing he did was look in the firebox. He then turned to me and said, "I told you to shake those grates." I said, "I did." He said, "don't lie to me." Being raised in the coalfields where it was the survival of the fittest, instinct was to hit him as hard as I could right in the nose. On second thought, I knew if I did, my railroading days would be over. The railroad did not permit fighting on the job regardless of whose fault it was or what the reason might be.

Not long after this I would get called to go out with the engineer that I had been with earlier on the double header from Cheviot to Peru. We were both working the extra board. He was on the engineer's board, while I was on the fireman's board. I guess he was one of the reasons I stayed with the railroad. He told me he really liked his job and that he was making $700.00 a month. In 1948, that was big money to me. At best, it was hard to get your rest and be ready to go, when you were on the extra board. You never knew for sure when you were going to be called. This particular night we were called around midnight for a westbound freight. Neither of us was married so with trying to mix irregular hours, social life, and being called in the middle of the night, we were both short on our rest. We had just left the yard in Peru when we were held in the sidetrack for an eastbound freight to enter the yard. On that cool night, with the heat coming off the boiler-head of the steam engine, we were both soon asleep. Neither of us woke up until the engine of the eastbound went by. We could both see on each of our steam gauges the situation we were in. I opened the firebox door to see only a faint glimmer of fire and a few hot coals. As the eastbound was entering the yard, he had to slow down, not to exceed fifteen miles per hour, as that was yard speed. This gave us a little more time. In short time we had the blower and stokers wide open and shoveling in coal with the scoop shovel at the same time. If we had not gotten ready to leave when we got the signal, we would have to explain the delay. The railroad didn't believe in excuses, not even good excuses. No way would they buy this.

 Another experience I had in the early days while working on the extra board was when I was called for a hostling job in Peru. This is a job that requires the fireman to move engines around the ready track, where the engines are placed to be worked on, supplied with sand, coal, and water. He was also required to move them in and out of the round house where they were taken for more complex repairs. The roundhouse was actually built in a portion of a circle so the tracks from each stall in the roundhouse could be matched up with the track leading onto the turntable located in front of the round house. Once the engine was on the turntable, the turntable was turned until it was aligned with the yard track the engine was to be put on. On this particular tour of duty, I had my first experience of trying to move a passenger type steam locomotive. It was setting in one of the stalls in the roundhouse. The shop foreman told me he wanted the engine moved a few feet forward. There were approximately four feet of space between the end of the tracks in the roundhouse and the metal lockers that set near the wall in front of them. I released the brakes, cracked the throttle open, but the engine didn't move. I opened it a little farther, but it still didn't move. Just as I moved the throttle the third time, the engine began to move and much faster than I had anticipated. At the same time, the mechanics scattered, having visions of the engine going through back wall. It actually happened to some other fireman, but luckily I was able to get it stopped and avoid an ugly scene. Also on several occasions, hostlers have backed engines into the turntable pit, due to moving the engine before the turntable was properly aligned. Fortunately, I never had that experience either. That was a rather serious mishap as the big hook (railroad crane for rerailing cars and engines) had to be called to lift the engine out of the pit. When an accident of this magnitude happened, the person responsible could be sure he would be called for a B of I (Board of Inquiry). The person charged could represent him self or be represented by another union member of his choice. The only advantage of being represented by someone else was if you were not satisfied with the decision of the B of I, you could appeal it to the labor board for a final decision. If the person charged was found not guilty, he could collect what he had lost in wages in order to attend the B of I. If found guilty, he might be given ten to thirty days "Overhead." If during this overhead time he got in any more trouble, he would have to serve the actual time given for that offense plus his overhead time. For more serious offenses, he might be given five days to a year actual time or be fired effective immediately. A young engineer who continued to have trouble running trains on the road would be restricted to yard service only or forced back to a fireman's position. Railroad tracks are divided into track sections called blocks, and the entrance to each block is governed by the color position of the signal at the entrance of the block. The color position of the signal gives the (signal indication) telling you how you will comply with that signal in operating your train. Signals had both a light (used for night operation) whose color determined the signal indication and a paddle, used for day operation, whose position gave the signal indication. Each signal pole contained two lights and two paddles, one directly above the other. Our signal colors on the Chicago Division were: green above red" Clear" indication was proceed at maximum authorized speed, yellow above red: "Approach." Approach next signal prepared to stop. All trains exceeding medium speed will reduce at once to that speed. Red above red "All Red." Indication was stop. Yellow above green- indication: Approach next signal at not exceeding medium speed. By not complying with these signals to the letter, an engineer could get in trouble very quickly. I had and opportunity to learn this very early in my railroad experience. It was the second or third trip I made eastbound out of Peru to Cincinnati. We were coming into Losantville where a sidetrack was located. We had an approach signal at the west end of Losantville, which meant we were to be able to stop short of the east end signal should it be red. The east end signal was about a mile away and around a slight curve to the left, so I had a better view of it than the engineer. This was at night so when the red signal came in sight, I called out, "All red," to the engineer. This section of track was on a slight down hill grade. I wondered why he didn't make an application of the air brakes in anticipation of stopping. Of course, since I was new on the job, I wasn't sure where the first application should be made and two that also depended on the length, weight, and speed of the train. I waited as long as I dared and called, "All red" again. At this time, he leaned out the window of the cab, where he could see the signal and immediately dumped the air. (He placed the brake valve in emergency stop position.) At this point, he read me the riot act for not calling the signal. I told him I had, but I suppose with all the noise in the engine, I hadn't called it loud enough. Forever after that, I made it a point to make sure I had been heard. When we finally got stopped, we were just a few car lengths from running into the westbound. He was supposed to have headed in at the eastbound signal but for some reason had run by the switch and the signal. He had got his train stopped, but hadn't been able to get it backed up behind the signal before we stopped in front of him. The signals were manually operated at this time. The dispatcher in Peru had no way of knowing what had happened, and of course, no one on either crew was about to tell. Nothing ever came of it. Had it became known, the westbound engineer who ran the signal, would have been fired, as it could have been a head on collision? In later years after automatic blocks when a train ran by a signal, the whistles and lights would have turned on in Peru telling the dispatcher what had happened. Though my engineer let me know right away he was a little upset with me, I believe if I had been in his shoes, with a new fireman, I would have kept a little better track of where my train was while running on an approach block.

There was another incident, that though it didn't start at Losantville, it did end there. I was called for a pool job east to Cheviot, Ohio. It had been raining in Peru that morning and just before we reported for work the temperature had taken a big drop leaving everything covered with ice. I arrived at the caller's office, read and signed the notice books. (This was required before every trip.) I then proceeded to the assigned engine and began preparing it for departure. Just as the engineer arrived, whom I judged to have been in his late seventies, I had climbed up on the engine, walked the long catwalk along the boiler, and was cleaning the small window in front of the fireman's seat. When I later got up in the cab, before he gave me a chance to introduce myself, he proceeded to chew me out. He said you could have fallen off that engine and gotten hurt. Then I would have had to make out an injury report. (I later found out he was the father of the Superintendent in Peru at that time.) Soon afterwards, we put our engine on the train and left town. Arriving at Losantville a few hours later, we headed into the sidetrack to meet a westbound that had not arrived yet. While we were waiting for him to arrive, the engineer got his oilcan and started down the engine ladder to oil around the engine. We had been running through freezing rain since leaving Peru, and the entire engine was coated with ice. Suddenly, having slipped on the ice-covered ladder, he disappeared from view. I ran across the cab and looked down the gangway. There I saw him lying on the ground about six or seven feet below. He had broken his fall by holding onto the grab irons as he fell. After seeing he wasn't hurt and after the way he had chewed me out in Peru about falling, I couldn't help but have a good laugh. He didn't think it was very funny at the time but he soon got over it.

During this period, while the C&O was running steam, trains were much shorter than in later years of diesel power. The diesel units were used in multiples on through freight runs. Due to these short trains, there were many more trains on the road and as the Chicago Division was a single-track road, you spent a lot of your time in a sidetrack waiting to meet trains or being run around by faster trains. While waiting in a sidetrack for several trains, (we called it waiting for the parade), I particularly remember one moon light summer night at Newkirk passing track. Newkirk was located at the top of Oakeann Hill approximately sixteen miles west of Cincinnati. Just west of Newkirk and east of the next station, Peoria, two steam engine powered trains had a head on collision a few years earlier. This collision resulted in the death of the engineer on one of the trains. Seeing there was going to be a head on collision, he jumped from the locomotive only to be run over by the cars of his train. There was a farm on the west side of the tracks at Newkirk. The farmhouse set approximately two hundred and fifty feet from the track. A farmer and his wife lived there. They also had a farmhand who worked there. When I came to the railroad in 1948, the story of what happened on the farm was told to me by several of the railroaders until I was beginning to believe it. Years later, while working an out post job at Burnham, Illinois, I ran across an old detective magazine that verified what the guys had told me earlier. Though I do not remember the exact year, I do remember it was in the forties. According to the men and the magazine, the hired hand and the farmer's wife had decided to kill the farmer. On the day of the Five Hundred mile race in Indianapolis, the hired hand drove to Indianapolis in time for the race and bought a ticket. He then rented a car, drove back to Newkirk, which is approximately a three-hour drive. After arriving at Newkirk, he hid in the barn with an ax. The farmer's wife then sent her husband to the barn, for some unknown reason. When the farmer entered the barn, he was killed with the ax. The farmhand and the farmer's wife then proceeded to put the body on the railroad track thinking a train would run over it. However, when they placed the body on the rail, they placed it on the first rail they came to which was the passing track. The next train that went through Newkirk went through on the main line instead of through the passing siding. This train did not hit the body and one of the crewmembers on the train saw the body on the other track. They notified the authorities and under questioning, the two were convicted of murder and sent to prison.

One occasion of being around a steam engine I'll never forget is when you would walk up to it and hear the low water alarm going off. This meant the water in the boiler was low. Should you climb up on the engine and check to see if there was any water showing in the sight glass? If there was, there was no problem. If there was not, another decision had to be made. If there was sufficient water in the boiler, you could add water and everything would be fine. If the water were too low when you started putting cold water in the boiler, again you would run the risk of blowing it up. The other alternative was to dump the fire out of the firebox, wait for the boiler to cool down, put the water in it, and rebuild the fire. This took considerable time and effort; this was the last resort. When an explosion, occurs, there is nothing more exhilarating than possible a head on collision between two airplanes in flight. On June 11 1953, my wife was working for a lady whose husband was a fireman on a C&O "mallet" (C&O largest steamer) arriving at the west end of the yard at Hinton, West Virginia. These big engines were used mostly over the mountain to Clifton Forge, Virginia, but some were used also down the river toward Charleston. On this particular day, as they arrived at the west end of the yard on engine No. 1642, the engine suddenly blew up. The entire cab was blown into New River that parallels the track from Hinton west until it joins the Kanawha River east of Charleston. The boiler was lifted off the frame and completely turned around. All three members were killed. The cause of the explosion has never been determined. There were some boys swimming in the river nearby, and they said all three crew- members were on the right side of the cab waving to them when the engine exploded. This meant the engine was not low on water, or the crew- members would have been busy getting water into the boiler, or possibly, the alarm was not working. In any case there is a sight glass on each side of the cab, most likely one of them would have seen it. There is another mallet, Number 1601, of this same type, in the Henry Ford Museum in Dearborn, Michigan.

All steamers had what was called "tires." These were outside rings approximately four inches thick, mounted on each driver. This was so the tires could be replaced instead of the whole driver, when being damaged, slipped, or spun, causing flat spots on the driver. I can remember many times hearing my dad complain when he would hear engine tires being slipped or spun, as it was the mechanical department that had to replace them and this meant extra work for him.

By this time I was beginning to realize you had to be a certain breed to like railroading, or at least like it well enough to not quit. Being called all hours of the day and night when you had only enough seniority to hold the extra board or pool jobs, being away from home on holidays, not knowing what it was like to sleep in your own bed each night, and having to stay at places like old Lady Warrens in Chicago. Many times I have awakened, and at first, not knowing where I was. I did relieve a little of the pressure by catching the Inter Urban and going to the museum on Lake Shore Drive in Chicago, and getting back in time to catch my job at 3:59 pm. The pay was great compared to anything I had had before. I enjoyed working outside and every trip was different. I met a lot of different people and made friends that I still have today. Also by now I was getting the hang of firing steamers, it was becoming second nature, like driving a car. This gave you more time to enjoy the scenery while watching for signals, objects on the track, defects in the track, and looking back on curves to observe any defects in the train. It was fun riding the steam engine, especially when it had just been overhauled, for then they rode good and looked great. I never got use to all the coal dirt associated with the steamers and cinders in my eyes. Today on the steamers specials, they wear goggles to eliminate the cinder in the eye routine.

One of the first things I learned was to carry more than one sandwich in my lunch. In those days they could keep you on duty for sixteen hours, and you might be stuck behind a wreck, or for whatever reason, and there wouldn't be a restaurant or grocery in miles. It wasn't unheard of, at this time, for a railroad crew to raid a farmer's cornfield and boil the corn on the boiler head for lunch-any port in a storm.

Retreat

I worked the rest of 1948 and through the winter, spring and summer of 1949. There were a few times I would be cut off a few weeks but not very often as there had already been several hired behind me. During these cut off periods, I would go back to West Virginia. The six guys I had always run around with were still there. I tried to get some of them to go to Indiana and hire out on the C&O, but they didn't want to leave West Virginia. It was one of those times I was down there; we rented a cottage on the Greenbrier River. We called it "The Bachelor's Retreat." We would throw parties on the weekends, special occasions or any occasion, inviting girl friends or whoever was handy at the time. The cottage was located about three miles from town and the city cops, who hadn't forgotten the problems we had given them over the years, would be around to check on us when we were coming back to town. One night, when they were chasing us, I turned in the C&O East Yard and waited until they passed. As far as I know, none of us were ever caught; at least I know I wasn't.

The Decision

In the late summer of 1949, I was back working out of Peru. On this particular night, I was sitting on a "Mike" at Burnham Yard, waiting for a "Highball" (permission to leave) with our train for Peru. For some time I had been trying to decide what I was going to do with my G.I. Bill. If I was going to use it to go to school, I should be getting started. Also, I had found out a railroad job could be lost very suddenly just by making a mistake or a miss judgment. If this should ever happen to me, I would need some other training to find work. By this time rumors were flying that the C&O was going to switch to diesel power. This was hard to believe, as the C&O had a lot of it's own coalmines. As I sat there, I decided I would get a leave of absence. That way I could hold my seniority, go back to West Virginia, go to school in winter, and come back to Indiana and railroad in summer. When I finished school four years later, and if the C&O had switched to diesels, I would come back, otherwise, I would go into another line of work. I liked the steamers, but I didn't like all that coal dirt. In September of 1949, I got a leave of absence from the railroad, went back to West Virginia, and enrolled in college. Concord, the college where I enrolled, was located at Athens, West Virginia about an hours drive from Hinton.

1950's

The next spring when summer vacation started, I caught the C&O passenger for Peru and marked up for work. Being one of the youngest men, I was still on the extra board working all different jobs, including out post jobs between Cincinnati and Chicago. Everything went well until about the second week in June, when due to a slow down in business, I was cut off. Thinking I would be marked back up in a couple weeks, I decided to look for other work in Peru and wait to be called back. I soon found a job with a construction company who was building a factory there in town. About a week later, my friend Frank Terry told me he had just had a wonderful idea. He and I should buy a Model A Ford and go to California in it. A Model A was a Ford automobile built between 1928 and 1932. At the time, my job wasn't too bad. We were making a cement floor for the factory, the pay was decent, and I figured I needed the money to help out with my schooling. My G.I. Bill was going to pay for only three and one half years, so I said, "No deal Frank." Just about every day Frank would come around and want to know when we were going to start looking for that Model A. One day I told him, "Frank, in the first place, I'm not going, and in the second place, if I were going, what do we need with a Model A? You already have a much nicer car." He said," I know but a Model A would be a lot more fun." About the third week on the job, I got transferred to a job unloading 80lb bags of cement out of boxcars. All of a sudden, Frank's idea of going west began to sound better. Soon, it was the only thing to do. After scouring the near by countryside, we heard there was a man who had one for sale that lived between Peru and Wabash. We got the directions and went looking. Sure enough he had not one but two. He said he would take fifty dollars for either one. One was a black Tudor 1928 and the other was a brown 1928 or 29 Victorian Model. When we told him we would take the Tudor and we were planning to go to California in it, he said he wasn't going to sell it to us. He said, "That car is worn out, a doctor owned it at one time and made two trips to Florida and back in it. After a long discussion, he finally agreed to let us have it, and we left for Peru. It rode like a farm wagon as it still had sixteen-inch wheels with the skinny tires on it. We replaced the sixteen-inch for fourteen inch, with wider tires, and had the valves ground. Frank's girlfriend's mother completely reupholstered the inside, we painted the wheels dark red, washed it, waxed it, and fixed the seats so the backs would lean back to make a bed. The fan belt on the car was frayed and though we found a new one behind the back seat, we decided to leave the old one on to see how far it would last.

West In The Model A

On June the 5th, 1950 at 9:45 A.M., we headed west on Route 24 out of Peru. We had groceries and a Coleman two burner gas stove. We also had curtains we could draw to cover the windows when sleeping. We slept in fields, behind billboards. in city parks, state parks, or where ever was convenient. One morning while cooking breakfast, Frank set a dozen eggs on top of the car. Not until we pulled out, did we realize we had forgotten the eggs but even then it was too late. The eggs were history. We had installed a temperature gauge in the middle of the dash. The night we spent in Yellow Stone it registered 40 degrees. The next day when running in the desert, it registered one hundred and fourteen. We took baths in lakes, rivers, showers, (if available) and in YMCAs, if there were any.

On July the ninth, we arrived in Casper, Wyoming. While we were stopped at a store a man who had seen our Indiana tags, told us he was from Richmond, Indiana. He said he and his family were having a picnic in a local park and asked if we would join them. Since we hadn't had any real food for a while, we were more than willing to accept. After the meal, the man's son and his girlfriend decided to take a walk. The park was very mountainous. Frank, who had never seen a mountain, wanted me to climb one with him. When we were approximately 200 yards up the mountain, our party began to yell at us to come back. When we got back down, they told us the boy and girl had walked under a cliff and someone, unknowingly, had shoved an 80 pound rock off the cliff striking Patty in the head. We carried her to the car and took her to a hospital. Though we had planned to leave the next morning, we stayed to see what Patty's outcome would be. On the morning of the eleventh, we were awaked and told Patty had died during the night. She was quite a loss. She would have been nineteen the next day. She was head of the musician's union in Casper, played in the Casper orchestra, and had finished high school in two years. Her father had run for Governor of Wyoming a few years earlier.

We made Yellowstone Park on the 12th, Reno, Nevada, on the 15th and crossed the Golden Gate on the 20th. The last time I had seen the Golden Gate was when I had passed under it on a troop ship coming home from service.

As Frank and I traveled westward toward Northern California, we decided we would drive up into the mountains to see some redwoods and maybe see some logging operations in the area. When we got up into the higher elevations of the mountains, it was a beautiful sun shinny day and everything was going great. However, this was not to last. While we were back on one of the unpaved logging roads, the Model A suddenly coughed and quit. You couldn't believe how quiet it got, and we were miles from anywhere, much less a mechanic. We knew without checking there should be plenty gas in the tank, but after looking the situation over, we determined that no fuel was getting to the carburetor. It couldn't be the fuel pump for Model As didn't have a fuel pump, as did later cars. The fuel tank set just below the windshield and above the engine, thus it was gravity fed. We started checking the fuel line from the tank to the carburetor. Inside the car, mounted on the firewall, I saw a small brass cut off valve, in the line. Yes, the valve was closed. Some big foot had hit it and knocked it closed. As I was riding in the passenger seat, and since the valve was located on the passenger side, it 's pretty obvious whom's big foot had hit it. Until this time, we never knew it had a shut off valve. Being where we were, we were very glad this was our only problem.

After spending a few days in Frisco and the Los Angles area, we decided we would get a job and stay awhile. Just a few days later the Korean War started, so I told Frank I would have to get back to Indiana as I would probably be called back in service.

At the tender age of twenty two, girls are rather important in a guy's life. However, having a twenty two year old car to offer for transportation, we didn't expect to be very successful in getting dates. To our surprise, they thought the Model A Ford was great, so for my first time, I went night clubbing in a Model A Ford and had a great time.

On the third day of August, we headed the ford east toward the Grand Canyon. Other than a few minor things, the car had done a fantastic job on the westbound trip. We had to have a small leak in the radiator fixed in Peoria, Illinois, where a passing car had thrown a stone into it. Farther west we had to have a radiator hose replaced. The man who replaced said, if we had enough nerve to start to California in a car this old he certainly wasn't going to charge us anything." The old fan belt made it to just over the California line. Just outside of Frisco one night, we locked the keys up in the car and had to break a window to get in. The next morning we drove across the Golden Gate Bridge, with one broken window, to get it fixed. Another problem we had, not with the car, was when we were crossing the dessert. We had tied two water bags on the front bumper. When we stopped for a drink, the rope holding the bags had broken, and the bags were gone. Until we got to a place where we could buy more bags, it got pretty thirsty.

On August 5th we made Yellowstone park, spent the day and left the next morning. Just after leaving St Louis on the 9th, the Ford started running rough but after making a few adjustments on the points it was as good as new. Approximately 2:30 pm on August 10th we arrived back in Peru. The Ford made the trip just fine. Frank didn't do quite as well. He ran out of money somewhere in the western states. To this day I don't know why I didn't leave him to parish in the dessert. At least that is what I tell him. As I would soon be leaving to go back to school, I sold my part of the ford to Frank. He later sold it to a car dealer, who in turn sold it to some Mexicans and they left for Texas in it.

I now stood for work on the railroad, so I went back to work, until time to leave in September for school. On the day I left for West Virginia, to go back to Concord College, the C&O brought a set of three F-7 diesels to Peru and parked them in front of the depot for the public to observe. They surpassed all of my expectations, both inside and out. They were nice to look at, very clean compared to a steam engine and the seats were as comfortable as any I had throughout the rest of my railroad career. The rumors were that the C&O would switch to diesels completely soon. My interest in railroading increased dramatically.

First New Car

I had been thinking about buying a new car before I left Peru. Due to the auto shortage after the war, you couldn't buy one off the lot. Your only chance was to put your name on a waiting list. When I got to West Virginia, I ordered a new Ford and two weeks later it came in. The total cost for a deluxe, the best that Ford made at that time, was $1749,oo. There is nothing quite like a young guy buying his first car, especially if it's brand new off the show room floor and paid in cash. After all those years walking across New River Bridge, especially in winter, I could hardly believe that car, in the driveway was mine. The bridge was only about two city blocks long but on cold winter nights, it seemed like six or ten.

My First New Car

1928 Model A Ford. This car was formerly owned by a doctor who made two trips to Florida and return in it. Frank and I drove it to California and back. I sold my half to Frank. He sold it to a car dealer who sold it to some Mexicans and they left for Texas in it.

Frank cooking breakfast.

Emergency Brake

The river bridge at Hinton consisted of four or five spans. At the end of each span was an expansion joint. As you crossed over these joints, the front tires of your car would hit them and make a noise. When you crossed the river from town and reached the other end of the bridge there was a ninety-degree turn to the left and straight ahead was a rock wall. My friends and I had a game we played. As we left town and hit the first span joint on the bridge, we would put the gas pedal to the floor and hold it until we hit the joint that connected the last span. (This was usually done late at night when there were no cops around, as we were sure they would frown on such a maneuver.) When you hit the last span, you had to be off the gas and on the brake or you would never make the curve. One night I was going through this procedure, my front wheels hit the last span, and I went for the brake. To my amazement, the brake pedal went all the way to the floor and there wasn't any brake at all. Through instinct, I grabbed for the emergency brake and was able to get slowed down in time. I found one of my brake hoses had ruptured and lost all of the hydraulic fluid. I saw a car one time that didn't make that curve and hit the wall instead. It wasn't a pretty sight.

Concord

Going to school at Concord was a fun time. It was located on a beautiful campus at Athens, West Virginia, approximately 15 miles from Bluefield. When the summer break came in the spring of 1951, I was cut off the railroad, so I went back to work at the dam in Hinton. As most of the carpenter work had been done, I went to work with the steel workers, who were installing flood- gates on the dam. A month or so later we were installing the side plates on the gates (these were plates to cover working mechanisms on the sides of the gates. They were approximately one half inch thick, 15 feet long, and weighed about 400 pounds) one of the plates was hanging from a crane on number nine wire. It was swinging gently about 15 feet above where we were sitting and standing as we ate. I heard a sound and looked up. The number nine wire had come loose and the plate was falling. Before I could say a word, it was down. It came so close to the Foreman, who was standing under it, that it tore the shirt on his shoulder and his pant leg as it fell. Though he only received scratches, he was just inches from being sliced like an apple.

We were all required to wear metal safety hats and when anyone dropped his, it went into the bottom of the lake at the bottom of the dam. Then you would have to go to the office, about a forty- five minute round trip, and pay for a new one. About three weeks after I had started working on the dam the first time, mine got knocked off and fell about two hundred feet into the lake. It landed upside down and was floating at the base of the dam. There was a big crane close by on top of the dam and though the operator couldn't see me, the guy relaying signals to him could. There was a chain connected on both ends to the hook of the crane. I motioned the signal- man to boom over to me-that I wanted to go down for my hat. At first he thought I was kidding but when I persisted, he boomed over to me, I sat down in the chain and rode down within one foot of the water and picked up my hat. That never seemed to catch on as a popular sport, but after that, anytime someone dropped a hat, they wanted me to ride the crane down to get it for them. I had several jobs while I was there: catching red hot rivets, in a small cone shaped metal container, bucking hot rivets, tying reinforcing steel, driving a pick up truck across the top of the dam, hauling parts, and etc.

Bar Stool

One night early in the fall of 1951, I saw, sitting on a bar stool, a girl I would later marry. I had stopped by Puckett's Drug Store with the intentions of picking up my girl friend, who worked at the soda fountain there, when she got off work. When I arrived, there was another girl sitting at the counter. She had come to pick up her aunt who worked there also. Soon everyone was introduced, as is the custom in a small town. Although I had never met her before, I had seen her a few times lately driving her dad's car around town. Her name was Pat and she worked at one of the local beauty shops. About a week later, I called her and asked for a date. She said yes and a year later, on September 8, 1952, we were married. On the morning of Sept. 8th, my dad and I were working on a paddleboat he was building to use on Bluestone Lake. This was the day Pat and I had planned to elope; I began to wonder how I was going to get away. Later on that morning we ran out of brass screws we were using on the boat, and my dad asked me to go to town to get some more. I said" Sure and soon Pat and I were on our way to Virginia, to get married, and on to Washington, D.C. for a honeymoon. (I don't know what my dad did about the screws.) Later that same month, I went back to school for my final semester. I had built up enough credits to graduate in January instead of May, although I wouldn't be able to get a second degree in teaching that I had worked for. In January of 1953, I got my degree and went to work for Hercules Powder Company in Radford, Virginia as a Foreman Trainee. Approximately one year later, the Korean War was over, government contracts were cancelled and I along with about 600 others was let go. I then went to work for a finance company in Arlington, Virginia.

In the fall of 1953 we had bought a new mobile home and were living in it at the time. With no experience pulling a trailer, I had a hitch made for my car, hooked it up, and headed across the Blue Ridge Mountains for Arlington. My car was only a 100 horsepower (1950 Ford.) If we had gotten stopped going up the Blue Ridges, we would probably still be there. Anyway, we made it to Woodley Hills Trailer Court, about two miles south of Alexandra on Highway 1.

I started to work for Household Finance Company as a Field Man and later became an Assistant Manager. I rather enjoyed the work and later after becoming Assistant Manager the air conditioned office was great. About a year later, when I learned more about the company and how they operated, I decided I didn't like working for them as well as I had previously believed. First they took away our forty hour week and told us we would have to work until the work was done with no overtime pay. On one occasion, I was working at the company office in Alexandra, when the manager took a weeks vacation leaving the Assistant Manager in charge while he was away. The Assistant had been there for quite some time so I'm sure he thought the Assistant was capable. On the day he returned to work, the Area Supervisor came the same day to make his three- month inspection of the office, as was their company policy. When the Supervisor decided the office hadn't been run to his expectations, instead of taking the Manager aside and instructing him as to how he should have handled the situation, in front of all the office staff, he told him he should take a few more days off and decide if he thought he could run the office properly. There was a saying among the employees, if you didn't have ulcers; you were not a good Manager. I knew there had to be a better way. A few months later, after I had made Assistant Manager and transferred to the Arlington office just outside of Washington, D.C., I received a letter from the C&O Railroad, saying locomotive fireman had been put on five day work weeks instead of seven, and they would no longer be able to give me a leave of absence. It was either go back to the railroad or give up my eight years of seniority. Knowing the railroad had switched completely to diesels, there was no decision to make, especially since I knew I would practically double my income. So once more we hooked up the trailer and headed west for Indiana. We arrived in Peru the following day after driving most of the night in the rain.

After passing my physical, I was given a book of rules, a time schedule, and manuals on the different diesels in service at that time. All the studying I had done on the steam engine manuals went out the window. Also now the Chicago Division over which we operated had changed from a manual block system to centralized train control. All main line signals were controlled by the dispatchers-located in Peru. Having been gone for six years, I had to make a trip east to Cincinnati and a trip west to Chicago to familiarize myself with the railroad, the new signals, and the diesels engines. I started making the familiarization trips during the last days of March 1956, however, I can only find records back to April, I, 1957.

On my first trip to Chicago, I was very pleased to find we were no longer staying at "Old Lady Warren's" place. We had been moved to the Rockwell Street Yard, approximately four to five miles west and we had a new dormitory to stay in.

I soon decided I had made the right move coming back. With the diesels the work was much cleaner, and they rode much better than the steamers. The Fireman's job was to keep all units, from one to five, working well, relay signals, look back on curves to observe the train, observe and learn the signals, the geography of the railroad, and to learn through observation and experience what would be expected of him in the future as an Engineer.

An F-7 nicknamed "Covered Wagon"

Working At Wards

In 1958 I was cut off the railroad, I went to work for Montgomery Ward in Peru. Years before, while still in high school during Christmas vacation, I worked for a clothing store so selling was not new to me. I worked in the paint and sporting goods department. The manager was Mr. Prange, a very nice man to work for.

One day a lady came in and told me she lived on a farm and wanted to buy paint for her out buildings. After quite a while, deciding just what kind of paint she wanted and how much of it, I wrote out an order, went to the basement, loaded it on the elevator, brought it to the loading dock and gave her the bill. She said" Oh my! I didn't know it would be that much. It is much cheaper in the catalogue." I told her "well, you would have to add the shipping charges on to that price and wait about a week for it to come in." She said "That might be, but I can't pay this much-my husband would kill me. "I had to load the paint back on the elevator and take it back to the basement.

When I hired out at Wards, I put on my application I had previously worked for a finance company. After I had been working there for sometime, Mr. Prange ask if I would like to do some credit work for them. I said, " Yes, be glad to." When I looked over their delinquent accounts, I couldn't believe what I saw. There were several large accounts that no payments had been made for months and no contacts had been made. Very little information had been gotten on the individuals when they took out the accounts. Now a lot of them had moved, changed jobs, or left town with no forwarding address.

I remember one of these accounts where this guy had bought a large storage building that had to be assembled after being delivered. No payments had been made in several months. I called, talked about their account, and they told me they would send in a payment. The payment didn't arrive, so I called again. When this payment didn't arrive on the agreed date, I went out to their house. A lady answered the door, and I told her I had come for the payment we didn't receive. She said, " I don't have the money." I said " In that case I will send a crew out to dismantle the building and take it back to the store. She said, " You won't be able to do that because it's all welded together." I went to take a look and there were no welds. I told her the crew would be out to get it and she best get her things out of it. She decided she had the payment after all, and we didn't have any problems with them afterwards. . I was soon bringing in chain saws, TV, etc. The fellow in charge of selling reprocessed merchandise soon told me " Don't bring in any more, I've got all I can handle." Soon afterwards Mr. Prange said the Wards Store in Kokomo had heard I had helped the Peru Store's Credit Department, and they wanted to know if I would work part time for them? I told him " I don't think so for now the railroad was calling me out in emergency (when the extra boards were exhausted they called cut off men) and that would be more than I could handle."

One day while working there, a friend who worked there also and I took two boats that belonged to the store to Lake Manitau. One was a twelve-foot fishing boat–the other was a forerunner of what now is called a wave runner. When we got to the lake, he got in the fishing boat, and I was on what appeared to be a motor mounted on skies. That dude would really go. After a while he wanted to trade and soon there after I looked up to see his boat going in a huge circle. The boats were scattering to get out of the way. My buddy had gotten thrown off and the boat was running wild. After what seemed like forever, it went through some weeds that stopped up the cooling water intake and caused the motor to over heat, seize up, and stop.

Another friend of mine at Wards was Al. Al would always have you laughing. There was a tavern just across the alley in back of the store. Al would make a few quick trips each day to boost his courage. One day while going over a ski jump in West Virginia during the late fifties, I broke a bone in my foot. As a result, I had a cast up to my knee and was walking on crutches. Later when I was able to go back to work, I told Al what happened, he really gave me a horselaugh. A short time later Al and his current girlfriend, whom he had been dating since back in the forties, had decided to get married. They bought a Mobile Home that was located in a Mobile Home park on the east side of town. They got married and were spending their wedding night in the Mobile Home. Al, who had been driving a 1955 Chevy Convertible at the time, parked it along side the mobile. That night a tornado went through the Mobile Home Park. During this time my wife and I were living in the house we were building though it wasn't completed. In the afternoon of the next day, I was working inside on some windows when I saw Al walk up to the back door. I couldn't believe what I saw. His entire head was wrapped with gauze, his nose was skinned and he was walking with a crutch. I said, "Al, what happened to you?" This was what he said, Jack you know we had a tornado last night? We hadn't been to town that day and the afternoon paper hadn't been delivered yet. All we had gotten was a little wind so we didn't know any serious damage had been done in the area. He said, "After we went to eat, we came home, parked the car next to the mobile, went in, took off all our clothes, and went to bed. We were lying there in bed admiring the beautiful woodwork on the ceiling, when the wind started blowing. I tried to close the window but because of extreme pressure, I couldn't get it closed. The next thing I knew the trailer turned upside down and I was sliding on that beautiful ceiling on my bare bottom." His wife didn't get any serious injuries. The trailer had turned upside down over the car and both were a total loss. After I knew he was o k, the way he told this story, and the way he had made fun of my broken foot, I couldn't help but have a good laugh. After fifteen years of dating, their wedding night was spent riding out a tornado.

Business began to pick up on the railroad and soon I was called back to work. Sometime later, Al and a friend of his were driving west on route 24 towards Logansport from Peru. During the trip, they had an accident in which Al was killed. I had many laughs with Al and, as a friend; I've missed him very much.

Forty Miles From Nowhere

After getting off work at Rockwell Street Yard in Chicago one day, a friend of mine who was a switchman there and who also lived in Peru, and I decided to catch No 92, a C&O fast freight home to Peru. To ride a train that you were not a crewmember of, company rules dictated you would have a message to ride. This message was received through the operator from the dispatcher in your home terminal, in this case Peru. As I had just gotten off work, I didn't have time to get a message before 92 would leave. As for my friend, I don't know why he didn't have one. I do know he had just gotten back from the local tavern. Judging from his actions, I would say he had spent quite sometime at the tavern. No 92 always made one stop to pick up cars from an interchange point, with another railroad on its run to Peru. When the train stopped to make the pick up, the conductor walked over from the caboose. When he got to the rear unit where my friend and I were riding, he climbed up into the cab. Since he didn't know either of us, he asked to see our message to ride. I told him I had just gotten off work before the train left and didn't have time to get a message. He said, " For your own protection, in case of an accident, you should have a message, and in the future, if you ride this train, you will have a message regardless of the situation." I know the conductor was trying to give us some good advice, but my friend, who was still feeling his booze, didn't take it that way. As the conductor was climbing down the ladder of the engine, my friend said, " I hope the S.O.B falls and breaks his neck." I thought to my self, oh no! He's going to put us off and we'll be forty miles from nowhere on either side of the train. Well I don't know whether the old boy couldn't hear well or if he just didn't hear because of the noise of the engine. Anyway we were lucky he didn't make a milepost out of us.

Lesson Learned

As mentioned before, fireman had to work as hostlers also. On these jobs a fireman was responsible for moving engines in or around the shop area so that they might be serviced or repaired. These jobs were bid in for one year at a time. When the regular hostler laid off, someone off the fireman's extra board worked the job. I bid this job in only one time for they were lower paying jobs. On this occasion, I was building my house and needed more time at home. There was one day on this job I will never forget. They had just installed a wash rack, similar to a car wash, so the engines could be run through for cleaning. The General Foreman, whom I was working for on this particular job, was anxious to show it off to the officials of the Nickel Plate and the Wabash railroads, who had terminals in Peru at that time. Usually, I was always at work ahead of time and always at least on time, but on this particular day, for what reason I no longer remember, I was a few minutes late. It probably had something to do with building the house. When I arrived the officials from the three different roads were waiting for me to bring the units through so they could watch the wash rack in operation. Two of the diesel units were coupled together. The other one was setting about twenty feet away on a track that led to the diesel house. Being in a hurry to get coupled up, I didn't have my helper check to see if this unit had a hand brake set on it. When I coupled into it, the knuckle that connects the two units, did not close, so the unit, from the impact, started towards the diesel house door, as it did not have a hand brake set on it. This was an automatic metal, folding door.

(Big bucks by any standards.) Luckily my helper was able to catch the unit and set the hand brake before it got away. Imagine the results had that unit gone through the diesel house door. Another lesson learned.

Cook Cars

Anytime there was a big derailment or wreck, the big hook (a huge steam operated crane used for re railing railroad cars and engines), had to be sent out and they always sent cook cars where the men could eat. The C&O always fed well on these cars. It was a treat to eat on these cook cars, for not only was the food good, but was always plenty of it. One night while at a wreck at Lacrosse, Indiana, (I was still a fireman at that time), I said something to the engineer about being hungry. He said" Go back to the cook car and get something to eat." I said, "It's only 3:00 am they are probably not open." He said, "If the cook is there, he will fix you something." I went back to the car and the cook was the only one there. I asked if there was a chance of getting something to eat? He said, "Sure, and fried up a skillet of bacon and eggs, which I finished off. About three hours later, they sent a relief crew and told us to go eat. We went back to the car, and I still remember, I ate six pork chops along with the rest of the meal. Though I don't eat like that anymore, I still miss those cook cars.

House

In 1956, we bought an acre of ground, on what was then highway 21 about four miles south of Peru. In 1957, we pulled our house trailer out on the lot and started building a house. There was an engineer whom I worked with that had built houses before he became a railroader. He said he and I could frame it up, so we went to work. In 1958, we moved in. It was livable but nothing was finished on the inside. Only sub flooring, no trim, and only one bathroom. It was three years before it was finished as I was away from home so much at that time.

A Wild Ride

While we were still running F-7 units, and before I was promoted, I was called out with an engineer who always seemed to have a dislike for me. I never knew why for I never did anything to him that I was aware of. One day on a previous trip, he accused me of something I hadn't done, and I let him know how I felt about that. I figured what I told him about evened up the score, but I guess he wasn't satisfied. On this particular trip, Number Ninety, Peru to Cincinnati, we didn't make any stops; they were all through cars for Cincinnati and as far as the East Coast. This guy had been known to work with a few drinks under his belt. I don't know if he had been drinking that night. At least I didn't smell anything on him. I believe his intention was to scare me, and if that's what it was, he got the job done, but I would never have let him known. Soon after we left Peru, he had the train running as fast as it would turn a wheel. He was going up and down hills, around curves like a wild man. Just east of Muncie, Indiana we came to a long, descending stretch of track, where the train would always pick up speed. Then you would pass under an overhead bridge and into a reverse curve that had a speed limit of 35 miles per hour. That night I kept waiting for him to make a brake application to start slowing the train down. Finally he reached for the brake valve and started drawing off some air. Just at that time, we passed under the overhead bridge. He realized where we were and that it was too late to brake for the curves ahead so he kicked off the air. We went around those thirty- five-mile an hour curves at approximately 50 mph. We were lucky to have made it at all. As we approached Economy, Indiana, we had to go through a down grade reverse curve and across a small bridge. I didn't know if we were going to make it, but I was sure glad we did. It was at this time I decided he would never pull that on me again. I would dump the air and then he could explain to the company why I had done so. Several years later, this same man got off the engine of a train he had brought into the terminal, walked across some adjacent tracks, and was run over by another engine, killing him instantly. Even though he gave me the wildest ride I ever had, I still hated to see him end this way.

1960's
Promotion

Usually when a fireman stayed on the job with the same engineer, that engineer would give him an opportunity to gain experience by running the train under his supervision. However, I was at the position on the seniority list where I could only hold the extra board and continually worked with different engineers. So the day I got promoted to engineer, I had never run a train on the main line. To say the least, this does place one at a disadvantage. I could have been called out in emergency, had the engineer's extra board been exhausted, to run a 100 car coal train with no experience. I brought this to the attention of the officials who had promoted us, so they put out an order that none of us would be called as engineer on the main line until we felt we were qualified. Shortly thereafter, due to an increase in business and retirements, I was able to get the necessary experience I needed.

I was soon to get my first lesson about running a train on the main line. Coming out of Cincinnati on a coal train, I was running for an engineer I soon became very fond of. Not only was he a likeable person but also a talented engineer. The company thought so to for every time they ran a test train (a different type of train than we were used to running on this division in regards to length, weight and etc), it was always called when this engineer stood to be called for the job.

Coming into Converse Cut, you first passed through a dip, then down a hill into a twenty mph curve, through an underpass and then back up an ascending grade. I had made a reduction on the train brakes earlier in order to slow the train down for the twenty mile per hour curve. However, when the brakes began releasing, the train began to pick up speed. We went into the curve at twice the speed we should have been going. The diesels were rocking back and forth, and I was quite concerned as to how this was going to play out. When I looked at the engineer to see how he was taking this, he smiled and said, "Bet you don't do that again." And you know, he was right.

Bad Weather

On April 16, 1961, I was driving back to Peru, Indiana from West Virginia. There were four to five inches of snow on the ground before I left West Virginia, and it was still coming down. When I was just east of Richmond, Indiana, the windshield wiper on the driver's side quit working. It was Sunday and all the garages were closed. I stopped in a gas station and ask the attendant if he could fix it? He said " sure." About an hour after he got under the dashboard, I heard a spring let go and parts fell to the floor. It was then I figured I was in trouble. I was right, for in a few minutes he said, "Sir, I don't believe I can do anything for you." From Richmond I drove approximately 80 miles through a blizzard. sitting on the passenger's seat so I could see through the windshield. At this time I saw a sign saying a bridge was out, and I would have to detour through Wabash, Indiana. This would be about 18 miles over and back out of my way. After making the detour, I found the turn off to my house would have been before the bridge was out. I got home around midnight, called the railroad, and marked up on the extra board. At 2:40 AM, I was called to deadhead to Chicago. As I walked through the living room of my house, I saw lights on the highway in front of the house coming through the drapes on the windows. When I drew the drapes back, I could see several cars, stuck in the snowdrifts on the highway. I thought to my self, well I've never seen a time I couldn't get to town if I wanted to. With that in mind, I headed out. As soon as I hit the highway, driving my 1953 Chevy work car, I could see I had made a big mistake, but there was no turning back. I had snow tires on the car so other than plowing through the big drifts I didn't have any trouble for the first three miles. Then I came up behind three vehicles stopped in the road. The first in line was a wrecking truck stuck in a drift. The next was a Coupe with an automobile engine in the trunk. Next was a big four door Oldsmobile. We all pitched in and helped get the wrecker out. That wasn't too bad for he had a shovel, but when he left, he took the shovel with him. The guy with the engine in the trunk had enough weight that he had no trouble getting started. Then there were two of us left. He got behind the steering wheel, and I began pushing the big Olds. After quite awhile, we finally got it through the drift and then we started working on mine. After a few minutes, my helper said, "Well, I'm called on the railroad so I've got to go." I said, "I'm called on the railroad too and you are not going anywhere until we get my car out." He said, "OK," and we went back to work. Later I saw we were not making much headway so I told him "Go on, no need for both of us to miss our runs." I finally put a chain on one wheel over the snow tire and was able to get out. What normally takes me five minutes to get to town, that night, took three hours and forty minutes. I found out later, the guy who wanted to leave me in the snow lives a short distance from me. Though I've talked to him many times since then, he has never mentioned it. I don't know if he remembers that night or if he just doesn't want to talk about it.

Drinking Water On Engines

Drinking water on steam engines was kept in metal cans of about two- gallon capacity. The can was kept in a metal lined box, filled with ice behind the engineer's seat. The top of this box was a cushion so it could also serve as a seat. With the coming of the diesels, the water was put in one- gallon glass jugs. These jugs were turned upside down on the top of an electric water cooler. The cooler itself held about another half gallon of water. Nearby was a paper cup dispenser. This arrangement was used for a number of years and worked very well. Years later the water was supplied on the engines in sealed plastic containers and kept in a small refrigerator, which was better by far.

Rest Room Facilities

There were no toilet facilities on the steamers other than make do. When stopped, you could head for the bushes. When running, the only choice was to go back in the coal tender. With the diesels, we had both water coolers and toilets. The first ones were not exactly state of the art. When they flushed, they dumped out on the track. Later due to environmental reasons, the stools were equipped with incinerators. These never proved very successful as they seldom worked. Later they went to chemically treated- holding tanks, which were better by far.

Heat In The Cabs

On the steamers, the cabs were heated by heat coming off of the boiler head and also from hot water heaters along the floor on each side of the cab. There were also draw curtains at the back of the cab that could be closed in cold weather. The first diesels had hot water heaters. On the road engines they worked very well. On the yard engines they were okay, except in very cold weather then you could not keep the engine temperature hot enough for the heater to put out very warm air. These engines had curtains that could be closed over the radiators but even that didn't work. The only solution was to put on as many clothes as you could get on before going to work. At one point they tried using electric heaters. These first models were not very successful but the later models were much more improved. Another thing that caused the old "Jeeps" to be cold were the cab doors didn't seal very well, especially if the unit had been wrecked. So in real cold weather, the first thing you did was to seal the doors with paper towels to keep the cold wind out. Even if the heaters were working good, if you had to do switching regardless of the weather, you had to have the window opened to see signals from the brakeman and that made it pretty breezy in the cab.

Working The Hill

After being marked up as engineer, in 1963, and being one of the youngest engineers, I was forced to go to Cincinnati to work yard and transfer jobs. These jobs at Cincinnati consisted of yard jobs, where you switched cars for eight hours, (these were called the Battlefield jobs. There were also transfer jobs that took trains to Stevens, Kentucky, just east of Cincinnati, jobs that switched industries in down town Cincinnati, and also Hill jobs.Hill jobs worked up and down the hill between Cheviot, (a suburb of Cincinnati), and downtown Cincinnati. This hill had a very steep grade and it took a lot of power to be able to pull a train up this hill. Four or five units were put on the head end and one or two more on the rear end. Baldwin Locomotives, of the 5500 series, were used as pushers as they were big and powerful at slow speed. Coal trains usually consisted of 100 to 110 cars, at 100 tons each. Also, on the hill, were some high bridges of approximately 200 feet or more. Shoving a train of this size up a grade this steep, over bridges this high, and with engines of this horsepower, gave an engineer a strong feeling of satisfaction. To become a successful engineer, on this hill could only be achieved by working with an experienced engineer who could pass along his knowledge to you by letting you operate under his supervision. Working during the winter of 1963 and 1964, on these jobs, I had to have my head out the window a lot watching for signals from the brakeman on the ground. On very cold nights this could be very uncomfortable. There were a few storm windows around (these were box windows that fit in the engine windows, that permitted you to see the brakeman's signals without hanging out the window in the cold.) These windows were on first come, first serve bases and there never seem to be enough to go around, so I decided to make one of my own. It was however of a different design. It was collapsible, making it easier to handle getting on and off engines, had a carrying handle, and tented glass to cut the glare. I used it many times throughout my railroading days on yard jobs, work trains, wreck trains, etc. It was unique in that it was the only one on the division other than the company issued ones.

Caboose used at Richmond, Indiana (In need of a paint job.)

It was on this hill, on one occasion, that due to brake failure or improper procedure, an engineer lost control of his train. He was fortunate he was near the bottom of the hill when it happened. But even so, he went around a 10 mph curve on a high bridge at 40 mph. Had one of the engines or cars jumped the track, the destruction would have been tremendous.

While working at Cheviot shortly after I was promoted, I was called to run as an Extra, engine and caboose only, to Okeann Hill, about 20 miles west of Cheviot. When we arrived, there was a C&O Caterpillar buried to the frame alongside the track. They wanted to see if we could hook to it with a big cable and pull it out. We were using an 1800 horsepower Baldwin Switcher. After hooking up, the Caterpillar operator got on the Caterpillar and started it up. I eased out on the throttle and with no strain or pain; the Baldwin pulled him out as if it were a toy. The power of those engines were unbelievable

Sights From The Cab

It was interesting as well as entertaining some of the sights you would see from a locomotive cab window. On an eastbound freight out of Peru between Muncie and Richmond, Indiana, I saw two birds, one chasing the other, as they flew along side the engine. We went by a farmer's pond and as the birds flew over the pond, the bird in front dove down toward the water and pulled out just before striking the water. The second bird flew straight into the water. Evidently he was watching the other bird instead of where he was going.

On another eastbound trip, a deer came running full speed across the track. Just beyond the track was a right of way fence. He hit the fence head on at full speed. The force of the impact threw him backwards about ten feet. Not to be deterred, he got to his feet, headed toward the fence again, jumped it, and was soon out of sight.

Coming through Muncie on a westbound trip one afternoon, I looked down the track to see a dog, about 60 feet away in between the rails, running straight towards the engine. Many times I've seen dogs try to outrun an engine but never towards it. Though I blew the horn, he never made any attempt to get off the track but continued straight ahead until he collided with the engine. This appeared to be suicide, though I don't know if dogs are in to that sort of thing.

Things You Don't Understand

We had a brakeman on our division, I would have judged to be in his late forties or early fifties at the time, and he had been on the railroad several years so he had enough seniority to hold a good job. What got into this guy I'll never know, but one night he attempted to burn down the building where we all slept on our layover at the other end of the road. I heard he and the manager there had a disagreement, and he probably had too many drinks at the time. Nevertheless, the company was satisfied he was the one who had set the fire, and though it was put out before any damage was done, he was terminated by the company and never got back to work.

Learning The Hard Way

Soon after I was promoted in 1963, I was called for a yard job in Burnham, Illinois. I had worked this job many times as a fireman. There was a standard procedure; go to work at 3:59 pm, switch out the cars that were in the yard, and then go to lunch while waiting for the Harbor Belt Railroad to make a delivery to us. Then we would go back to work and switch out the cars for No. 90, a hot manifest, going to the east coast.

When going to lunch, we would run the engine down to a switch that led to a stub track along side the cars where we stayed while working there at Burnham. When stopping at the switch, the fireman would get off and throw the switch. The engine would then be pulled through the switch; the fireman would then realign the switch and get back on. We would then proceed another 100 feet to the camp cars. Approximately another 50 to 60 feet the track ended with a bumping post. After going through this routine for years, when I would be working at Burnham, I decided there must be a better way. (These ideas come to those who are young, foolish and inexperienced.) On this particular night I didn't have a fireman working with me. My idea was to stop the engine back of the switch, put the throttle in number one position, jump off, throw the switch, wait for the engine to pass through the switch at slow speed, then I would throw the switch back over and run and catch the engine. Sounded like a winner, at least at the time it did. I stopped the engine, put the throttle in no 1 position, jumped off and threw the switch. When about half of the engine had gone by me, I could see it was gaining speed much too quickly and by the time it would clear the switch, and I would have realigned it, I would never be able to catch the engine and get it stopped in time. I started running as fast as I could in the ballast rock along side the track. When I leaped for the grab irons, on the front steps of the engine, my right knee hit the corner of the metal steps. There was absolutely no give to the step and the pain from the impact was so severe that I was instantly sick all over. I couldn't move my right leg, but I knew I had to get up those steps so I dragged it behind me. Finally making it up to and across the cab, I put the engine brakes in emergency and the engine stopped before going through the bumping post. To say I wasn't a little apprehensive would be a lie, to say I learned a lesson would be absolutely correct. As it was in those days, you learned a lot by experience. After completing this tour of duty, I was relieved by the regular engineer on this job and returned to Peru to mark up on the engineer's extra board.

First Trip As Road Engineer

Shortly thereafter I was called for my first trip as an engineer on a road job. I was called for 4:10 am, on no 95 out of Peru for Chicago. My fireman was Bill Meadows, who also grew up in my hometown of Hinton, West Virginia. Though you are always sure everything will go wrong on your first trip, as engineer, I have no bad memories of that trip. We were called for no 90 on the return trip to Peru.

During my first year on the engineer's extra board it was pretty tuff because about every third call was a dead head to some outlying point. There you would work a yard or transfer job and it could be for one day or up to fifteen days. I remember on one occasion I had three calls in a row for deadheads, so during this time, I was gone a lot.

Truck Door

My wife, my two sons and I left Peru early one morning driving to West Virginia to visit some of our relatives. The fog was very thick that morning. It had just turned daylight when we arrived at a tee road just west of Muncie, Indiana. Though I had driven this road many times, due to the heavy fog, I almost drove through the tee. A mile or so east of this intersection was a C&O crossing. When we arrived there, a train was passing over this crossing so we waited for it to pass. When this train arrived at Peru and was passing by the yard office, someone saw a truck door hanging on the side of one of its boxcars. It was later determined that the truck had run into the side of the train, the same train we had waited for at the crossing near Muncie a few days earlier. After hitting the train, the truck had been dragged down the track for a ways thus no one could see it from the crossing. I no longer remember the outcome of the driver of the truck. In any case, it was very unusual for a vehicle door to hang on the side of a train after a collision.

Doley

An engineer, who was just a few men ahead of me on the seniority list, was westbound out of Peru with a coal train headed for Chicago. Just after passing under a highway bridge, his train started to derail; a state policeman had stopped on the bridge and was watching the train pass when it started derailing. When the train stopped, he went to the locomotive. The engineer, whom we called Doley, said (" The first thing the policeman said was do these trains do this very often?) A few days later I was talking to Doley and I asked him if he had received any injuries? He said he was bruised up a little but otherwise OK. I asked if he had been to a doctor for a check up? He said no. I urged him to do so but he said he was all right. A short time later he was dead from internal bleeding.

Expensive Mistake

Mistakes are made everyday in every industry. Some of these mistakes are expensive some are not so expensive, and I suppose there are some that cost nothing at all. However, the mistake I am referring to was very expensive. Whenever your train has a high or wide load in it, the dispatcher is supposed to route your train over a track that will accommodate it. At least that is the way it is supposed to work. Before the engineer departs the yard, he will be given a message informing him of the high or wide load in his train. It is then the responsibility of the engineer to see that his train follows the given route for his train so as to avoid any low bridges or close clearances that his train will not clear. This particular episode, I am referring to, happened in the Chicago area several years ago. A train, carrying several cars of new Cadillacs, went under a low bridge. The top row of automobiles on the carriers immediately became convertibles as the tops were ripped off of them. I do not know who was held responsible for this fiasco. It could have been the dispatcher for not routing the train properly, or the engineer for not going as routed. In any case, some person or persons were in deep trouble. Cadillacs never did come cheep.

An Experience

Years later, when the C&O started moving grain trains eastbound, we would find Cheviot Hill to be quite a challenge to go down as it had been going up with the coal trains, for the grain was just as heavy as the coal. At least, you couldn't tell the difference. Usually if an engineer made a safe trip down the hill with a grain train, it depended on how he made the approach to the hill. These trains weighed approximately 10,000 tons. Any misjudgment or wrong procedure with a train this heavy on a hill this steep, and you are soon in big trouble. When we started running grain trains down Cheviot Hill, I was fortunate to have had previous experience on the hill. It made it a lot easier to adapt to the heavier trains. At this time we were using "stretch braking." I would start over the top at 7 to 8 miles per hour and make a 3 to 4 pound reduction on the trains airbrakes. When approximately twenty cars in the train had started down, and the train's speed was approximately 10 mph, I would make another reduction of 8 to 9 pounds. By the time the entire train was on the hill, it was stretched out, and I had reduced the throttle from #8 to #4 or # 5. With this setting, unless there were bad air leaks, I could usually make it to the bottom of the hill with out further adjustments. When we started running these grain trains, we had a Road Foreman, who was in charge of the engine crews when in the Cincinnati area. I am not sure how this man ever got an officer's job. Though he was a nice guy, on the job he was a pain. He was long on instruction but short on skill. At this time the company did not want you to wear sunglasses or earplugs. Having been use to wearing sunglasses, when flying airplanes, it did not seem right not to wear them, or ear plugs for that matter, so I wore both of them. Thus "Twiggy" (what we called the Road Foreman, as he weighed around 250 lbs.), and I were at odds on various occasions. When an engineer ran his first train down Cheviot Hill, a road foreman was required to ride with him in order to qualify him, as to proper procedure to use in this territory. On arriving at Cheviot one day and knowing "Twiggy" would be riding with me, I decided to have some fun and at the same time get even with "Twiggy" for the harassment he had given me in the past. When I stopped at Cheviot to pick him up, I immediately got out of the engineer's seat and set down on the other side of the cab. When "Twiggy" came up in the cab he said, "You go ahead and run it." I said "I would feel safer if you would show me the proper way to handle this train down the hill." (He didn't know I was already qualified on the hill.) When he sat down in the engineer's seat, I went over, got my jacket and suit case, and moved them over close to me, which ordinarily I wouldn't have done. The fireman, sensing something wasn't right said, " Jack, what are you doing?" I said, " If it looks like this train is going to get away from him, I'm going to unload." He said, " Are you serious?" I said, "You bet I am." He said, " Well me two." We did make it down the hill but not until we had gone into emergency three times. When I saw the Conductor and Flagman at the terminal, they were fit to be tied. They said," What were you trying to do, kill us." (They had been on the caboose.) I said, " It wasn't me running the engine, it was "Twiggy." They said," We thought so." The conductor immediately went to the phone, called the Superintendent in Peru and told him if "Twiggy" was going to be running our train down the hill, he was going to get off at Cheviot. (He thought it was "Twiggy's" idea to run the engine.) When I ran into the Superintendent later on, he said, "Jack, please don't let "Twiggy" run your engine anymore." I never did.

Should Have Known Better

One night while we were still running F-7s, I was called for a run to Cincinnati. I reported for work a little early, stopped in the caller's office to read and sign the bulletin books, and then went to the ready track where our engines were setting. The engineer had not arrived yet, and while I was checking the engines and supplies for departure, the head brakeman came up on the engine. He said something to me twice, but as his speech was slurred, I didn't understand him and didn't make an answer. He then proceeded to get off the engine. Shortly thereafter, the engineer arrived and wanted to know if the head brakeman had shown up yet. I told him he had been there but had gotten off the engine without saying where he was going. I looked the local area over but found no trace of him. I told the engineer I would line the switches, so we could get our engine to the other end of the yard and on our train. Maybe by that time he would show up. Sure enough, after we had gotten on our train and ready to leave, he came up in the cab. He started complaining because we didn't wait on him and made him have to walk from the ready track to the other end of the yard where our train was located. I realized it was a pretty long walk, but we were already late getting our train out because of him. The engineer told him to set down and keep quiet. With that, the engineer released the brakes and we started pulling out of the yard. Before we had moved a hundred feet, the brakeman started complaining again. The engineer stopped the train, called the yardmaster on the engine radio and told him to call another brakeman because he wasn't going to take this one any further. If he would just have kept quiet, everything would have been fine, but by opening his mouth one more time, he lost his job. He was pulled out of service, called for a board of inquiry and fired for Rule G (drinking on the job). He was a middle-aged fellow with years of seniority: he should have known better.

Doubling Hills

Many times when climbing hills with maximum tonnage trains, you don't make it to the top. This can be due to engine failure, sanders becoming stuck or running out of sand, being overloaded, or numerous other reasons. When you reach the point where you are stalled, the head brakeman goes back and cuts off about twenty cars. You then proceed to the first passing track, when you are operating on single track as we were doing. The cut off cars are then pulled to the far end of the passing track, just to clear the signal. The engines are cut off and pulled out on the main line beyond the switch. When you receive a favorable signal, you return to the remainder of your train that had been left on the hill. At this point, the train is coupled up and pulled down beside the cars that had been cut off in the passing track. The train is cut off just behind the signal and the engines are pulled up over the switch. The switch is lined for the passing track; the engines are backed in on the cut off cars and are pulled out over the switch. The switch is aligned for the main line, the engines, and cut off cars, are backed on the train. The air hoses are coupled up, an air test is made, and then you call the dispatcher for permission to leave or you back your train back of the signal and wait for a permissive signal to proceed. Though this was standard procedure used by the railroads, it was nonetheless expensive for the company as it was time consuming, and the crews had to be paid for the extra miles run while making the double, (this move was called "doubling the hill".)

Wreck On The Bridge

By mid 1964, the F-7s (nicknamed "Covered Wagons") had begun to thin out being replaced by 5900s, 6000s and 6100s, built by General Motors and nicknamed "Jeeps". I hated to see the F-7s go, but the jeeps were better for switching, especially on a cold winter night. Visibility for switching was much better.

During this time, it seemed as though you never had enough power. You would be given tonnage trains (maximum tonnage for the amount of power you are using,) and if the sanders didn't work properly, you didn't stand a chance of making the first hill out of town. This was soon to change with the coming of the 7400s. These were fantastic engines, built by General Motors with 3000 horsepower. Not only did we have the needed power, but also we had to run the trains differently. Before on the up grades, we were always running at full throttle. Now, sometimes on the upgrades, you had to reduce the throttle. Also before with the older units, if you didn't have your train bunched, (slack removed between each car by backing cars up tight against each other), the engines might not be able to move the train. Not with the 7400s- when you opened the throttle, either the train moved or it pulled apart. The 7400s could run a coal train like a passenger. We called them the Cadillacs because they were so powerful and road so well. Our good fortune was not to last. After a couple of derailments, one a very serious accident, the 7400s were pulled off of our division. The officials said the three wheel trucks, the 7400s had, would not slew properly around some of the tighter curves on the Chicago Division. Several years later however, the 7400s were returned to the Chicago Division. The most serious accident occurred just east of Richmond, Indiana, in 1965. The train had stopped at Richmond to pick up or set off some cars and then continued eastbound. Approximately two miles later they entered a turn to the left and then out onto a high bridge. The 7421 was in the lead, 7425 was the second unit, and 7428 was the last unit. The third brakeman was riding in the second unit. He was a young fellow, who had just recently hired on with the C&O. As the 7421 went out on the bridge, the crewmembers on that unit felt it raise up and then come back down on the rails. Suspecting there was something seriously wrong, they continued on across the bridge before stopping, as it was at night, and they couldn't see what was happening behind them. When they went back to investigate, they found the 7425 had rolled off the bridge and landed upside down on a cement pier that had been used for the previous bridge there. The brakeman, who had been riding in the 7425, had been killed in the fall. The 7428 had derailed along with 15 to 20 cars and rolled down the embankment. The 7428 had also caught on fire and was burning. About a day later, I was called for a wreck train to go pull the 7428 out. Both the 7425 and the 7428 were returned to General Motors to have new bodies put on them. Sometime later, I was at the west end of Peru Yard, preparing to depart on a westbound freight when I noticed in my engine consist a unit that looked like a 7400 but didn't have a 7400 number. However, when I checked the identification plate on the frame, it was one of the engines that had been in the wreck on the bridge at Richmond and had been renumbered.

#7428 near camera, after fire.   # 7425, where brakeman was riding, in background.

No. 6319 holds the main for two opposing trains. It is showing the Chessie System logo used prior to changing CSX

What!

In Chicago in the sixties, there was very heavy train traffic and tracks were running all over the city and suburbs. One day shortly after I was promoted to engineer, I was working a yard and transfer job in Chicago. The other members on the crew were recent hires so none of us were familiar with some of the tracks around the city. This particular day, the yardmaster, who was a likeable guy but somewhat short fused, told us to make a delivery to the North West Railroad Yard. Well, though I still don't know for sure how it happened, when we left the yard the engine was headed east. (Where we were using the engine in the yard, it had to be facing east so the engineer could see the switchman's signals.) When we got back and the yardmaster saw the engine he immediately came unglued. He wanted to know how we got that engine turned around and of course, we couldn't explain it. We finally had to take the engine to another railroad yard where there was a wye track so we could turn the engine back around.

Unscheduled Meet

With every crossing you came to there was always the possibility of a collision with cars, trucks, people or whatever, and the Chicago Division had lots of crossings. I was coming westbound through Marion, Indiana when a 1949 or 1950 chevy tried to beat me over the crossing. Three fourths of the car made it, one fourth didn't, as I got him in the left rear fender. When I hit the car, the trunk lid flew up and golf clubs flew out all over the road. He stopped the car, jumped out, gathered up the golf clubs as quick as possible, jumped back in the car and took off. There were all kinds of strange noises coming from the car as he sped out of sight.

A few years later, I was westbound at night coming into Converse Cut. This was a railroad bridge where the C&O tracks passed under the Pennsy tracks. As I came around a curve, I could see someone standing on the crossing approximately a city block ahead, waving his arms. Though all I could see was a man in a white tee shirt, I put the brakes in emergency. As we got closer, I could see a car setting on the crossing. However, part of the train was on a down hill grade so no way could we get stopped in time. Just before the impact, the fireman, head brakeman, and I ducked down to avoid flying glass and automobile parts. After the collision, I raised up to see us pushing the car down the track ahead of us. When we came to a small bridge, seventy to eighty feet later, the car went off into the creek, and we stopped shortly thereafter. We got off the engine and went back to be of assistance to anyone who might have been injured in the car. When we got back to the car there was no one in it so we walked back as far as the crossing looking under the train and still found no one. We called out but no one answered. I saw a house across the highway so I went over to call the sheriff. As I was walking back, I thought I heard voices coming from some bushes nearby. I walked over to the bushes and shinned my light into them. There sit two men. I asked if the car belonged to them? One said, "It belongs to my wife and she just bought it today." It had been a very nice car, two tone green, brand new Plymouth but the only trip it would take now would be to the junk yard. The driver lost his glasses and he asked if I was going to take him home, and if not, he was going to cause me some trouble. I said, "Don't worry about it, I've got a ride coming for you. Little did he know it was the sheriff.

Kids On The Bridge

After coming down Okeanna hill, going east towards Cincinnati, we would go around one or two curves, and then go over Miami River on the railroad bridge. After we rounded the curve, it was a short distance to the bridge. Since the rear of the train was still on the hill, we were usually running pretty fast. Numerous times we would come around the last curve to find a bunch of "hippies" on the bridge. I never figured out what the attraction was but every now and then they would be there. I never heard of any of them being hit. They would always run to get off the bridge when they heard us coming. One day I came in sight of the bridge and there was still one boy and girl running for the other end of the bridge. The others had already gotten off. The boy had the girl by the hand and was pulling on her trying to get her to run faster. From watching her, I would say she had never had much experience running on railroad bridges as he was practically pulling her off her feet. Their luck held and they were able to make the other end. I don't know about the boy but I bet that girl never got on a railroad bridge again.

Cement Truck

While on an eastbound freight out of Peru for Cincinnati, we were approaching Cottage Grove, Indiana running about sixty miles per hour. As the signal tower came into view, I saw what looked like a vehicle sitting on the crossing near the track. As we got closer, I began blowing the horn expecting the vehicle to move. By this time, I could make it out to be a very large ready mix cement truck with several people near it. Instead of the truck backing off the track, it stayed there and the men ran from it. I put the brakes in emergency and at this time one of the men returned to the truck, jumped up on the running board, as if to enter the truck, and then turned his head and looked toward the train. Then instead of getting in the truck, he jumped off and ran. We braced for the impact; however, we missed the mixing barrel where most of the weight would have been, and instead tore off the rear bumper and the operating equipment located on the rear of the truck. As heavy as a loaded cement truck is, a collision with one would be disastrous for the truck, anyone in the truck, and also for the engine and engine crew.

Save The Battery

One night we were on a run on a fast manifest train just west of Shandon, Ohio, approximately sixteen miles west of Cincinnati. As we came around a left hand curve, I saw a car's headlights shining straight at me, and the car was sitting in the middle of the track. Though I put the brakes in emergency, we were much too close to stop. We hit the car at a high rate of speed and though I ducked down below the windshield, as I looked out, after the impact, I saw the car going straight up in the air. It went end over end as if it had been place kicked like a football. By some miracle the car, or the remains thereof, came down on the highway at the crossing. We searched for the occupants of the car, but found no one. While searching, I heard someone singing as he walked down the road. As he approached me, I asked if the car belonged to him? In a highly intoxicated voice, he assured me it did. Though the car was completely destroyed, by some miracle, the left tail- light was still burning. He walked to the car and tried to stick his head into the remains of it. I asked, " What are you doing?" He said, " I'm going to turn out my lights to save the battery.

What Will I tell My Husband?

On the return trip from Griffith, Indiana (just east of Chicago,) we had just passed north Judson, Indiana, when I saw something on the track a head. It was still too far to make out what it was. The time was around 11:00 pm. I could see it was not moving, so I started blowing the horn. As we got closer, I could see it was a car or truck. As I put the brakes in emergency, I couldn't see anyone and the vehicle still wasn't moving. As we didn't have time to stop, we hit the vehicle cutting it in half. It had been a very nice, full sized, like new Ford Station Wagon. It was white with wood like trim on the sides. We had a short train so when we got stopped; the caboose was close to the scene of the collision. I called the caboose, told them what we had hit, and they walked over to the crossing. When they arrived, they found a woman standing by the right of way fence. She told them the car belonged to her and her husband. A man soon arrived and said he had gone to find a tractor to pull the station wagon off the crossing but had not been able to find one. The crossing that the wagon had been sitting on was a private crossing that only went into a farmer's field. A track gang had been working on the crossing that day and had removed the ballast from it, so when the couple started to cross, they got hung up on the rails. As the caboose was near, the conductor asked them to go to the caboose to make out an accident report. As they gave their names and addresses, it became apparent he was her boyfriend-not her husband. As the boyfriend looked around the caboose he said," This is the first time I have ever been on one of these." She was somewhat less impressed with the caboose and in between crying jags she said, " What am I going to tell my husband?" I've often wondered what she did tell her husband.

People I worked With

Occasionally I think back of people I have worked with. One person that comes to mind we called "Huge." He was a big man, set in his ways, and well known by everybody on the division. If "Huge" didn't like you, he would give you a hard time. When he was an engineer and I a fireman, we had a few run-ins. One day we got into it on the job and before it was over we had an understanding. After that "Huge" was a different man with me and we got along fine. In fact I found he had a great sense of humor, and I enjoyed working with him. One day while he was still an engineer, we were going by the train order office at Cottage Grove, Indiana, on a hot train. As we were traveling at high speed, he missed the orders as he reached to grab them from the hoop. I was standing behind him and when I saw he had missed them, I looked back and saw one of the crew members on the second unit, had gotten their set of orders. I told him they had gotten their orders and if there were anything important, they would let us know. He taught me a lesson, one I would never forget, real fast. He said," I don't care if you are working with Jesus Christ, you read the orders yourself." Of course he was telling me this for my own good and it probably kept me out of trouble later on. Another time, when I was still a fireman and working with him, I got off the engine before we left Peru to get a jug of water. When I came back, I had to cross a track to get to the engine. It was at night and as I crossed the track, a yard engine, without any lights on was coming and I couldn't hear it for the noise being made by our own units. At this time "Huge" yelled to warn me and I was very grateful he did. In later years, "Huge" lost his engineer rights due to medical .

Excitement To Spare

Strange things sometimes happen in the cab of a locomotive as it did on this occasion. An eastbound freight was called out of Peru for Cincinnati. Due to a train wreck at the bottom of Oakeann Hill, this freight was instructed to set their train out at Medford, Indiana and go east with only their three units and caboose. The crew consisted of the engineer, fireman, head brakeman third brakeman, flagman and conductor. The engineer, though a very likeable person when sober, was hard to get along with when drinking. Prior to leaving on this trip, he had been drinking pretty heavily though the company officials did not know it. When setting the train out, though not known by the other crewmembers, the engineer had cut out the air that operated the brakes on the engines. When they started down Oakeann Hill their speed continually increased. In the meantime, the engineer got upset with the head brakeman, got up out of his seat, walked across the cab, swung at the brakeman, missed him, and hit the fireman sitting behind him knocking him out. The third brakeman, back on the third unit, tried to cut the air in the third unit in order to get the brakes to work but couldn't do so. He then made his way to the head unit and cut the air in there. By this time the engines were far exceeding the speed limit and rocking so bad they were throwing ballast. As soon as the air built up, they put the brakes in emergency and stopped just short of the wreck that had occurred there on the hill. This could have been a real disaster.

Meeting eastbound 7086 at Hoover, Indiana

Lost

On a hot manifest run from Peru to Cincinnati, we were going through Boston, Indiana, when I told the fireman he could run the train. Firemen were permitted to run trains, under engineer supervision, to give them experience in preparation of becoming engineers. This fireman had been on the railroad over three years and should have had, at that time a pretty good knowledge of the geography of the railroad and the location of signals. About twenty to thirty minutes later we reached the top of Oakeann Hill. At this time, we could see the east end signal showing "approach." This was the same location where two steam engines had a head on collision years before. The "approach Medium" signal says you will approach the next signal at medium speed. The "Approach" signal says you will approach the next signal prepared to stop not to exceed thirty miles per hour. As we approached the first signal, I waited for him to make an initial reduction on the air brakes as this was all down hill and it was a short block. When he didn't make a reduction, I told him to make one. By this time, he should have made at least a ten pound reduction but instead he made about half that. The third signal would be only a short distance down the hill around a curve. If it were red, which it could be, we would have to be able to stop short of that signal, as there could be a train sitting just beyond that signal. Again I told him to draw off some air and again he made a short reduction. I knew we couldn't wait any longer. I made a leap for the brake valve, and threw the brakes in emergency. When we got stopped, we were only a short distance to the signal and it was all red. I asked him, "What were you trying to do?" He said, "I don't know," and I don't believe he did although being around as long as he had, he certainly should have.

Break-ins

While working a yard and transfer job out of Rockwell Street Yard in Chicago one night (These were jobs that did yard work and were also used to make pick up and deliveries from other yards in the area) we were instructed to go to downtown Chicago, switch out the freight house, and then on the return trip, stop and pick up a load out of an industrial track. When we stopped to pick up the car, we coupled into it and the brakeman walked down to make the coupling, let off the hand brake, and cut the air in the car. He quickly returned to the engine and said the car had been broken into. We got off the engine and went to look at the car. We had scarcely arrived at the car, when Chicago City Police surrounded us. They began asking questions as though we might be the ones breaking in the car. I wondered where they had been and how they arrived so quickly without us seeing them. As a matter of fact, what were they doing in this isolated area at that time of night? I had heard on more than one occasion of policeman being involved in boxcar break-ins in the Chicago area during this time.

Leaving Chicago with a hot merchandise train in the late sixties and early seventies was akin to running the gauntlet. The local thieves knew the location where all eastbound trains had to stop at a stop board before passing through the connection. They would work in groups. When a train left the yard, if for any reason it got slowed up to where they could board it, they would proceed to get the door opened and start unloading the merchandise as soon as the train stopped at the a stop board. If it were something unbreakable they would unload it while the train was moving. Though the railroad had at least one special agent working around the clock, they never seemed to have much luck breaking up these operations.

Comments On Some Engines Used

I ran my first 3800 series unit by General Motors on December 1, 1967, when I was called for second 95 from Peru to Chicago. The engines were 3856, 3858 and 7450. We had just started getting units of the 3800 series. They were new and very nice units, but they were only 2000 horsepower, not as big as the 7400s, and only had two wheel trucks. If I ever hated a unit to switch with, and I think I did, it was the 2500 series made by GE. It had a monstrous throttle that had sixteen positions and was an absolute bear to switch with. I'm sure whomever designed them is not, nor never has been, a locomotive engineer. I never developed affection for the B&O units of the 3000 series either. They had begun to mix the B&O and C&O units, so occasionally one would appear in the consist. These units were 2250 horsepower and very bad to slip the drivers. If you didn't have good sanders, you were in for a long day. Another series of the B&O units I would sometimes get, was an old style jeep that had the controls set up to operate with the long hood forward. Practically 40% of your forward vision was cut off. The horn was operated with cables hooked to the horns on the other side of the cab. It usually took both hands to pull the cables that operated the horns. If it hadn't been for the fact that I needed the money so badly at the time, when I saw one of these units was on the head end of my consist, I would have turned around and gone home. Another unit we used, usually with coal trains, that was rather unusual, was the 1800 series built by General Motors. Although they were new and powerful, they had been built on old 5500 series Alco frames. They rode like farm wagons. They were later renumbered to the 7300 series.

You've Got Three Minutes

While on a westbound freight out of Peru for Chicago, I saw what appeared to be a car on the crossing ahead of us that wasn't moving. I made a brake application to slow the train in case we had to stop. As we got closer, I could see the people in the car. At this time I made another brake application and stopped the train just short of the crossing. The right wheels of the car had missed the crossing and were hung up on the rails. I walked over to the car where three men were sitting in the front seat. From the odor coming from the car, I could tell John Barley Corn was involved, though I didn't see any cans or bottles insight. I asked them what their intentions were as to removing the car from the tracks. One of them said, "We are going to sit here until someone comes along that can pull us off." I could see that with a little effort, they could remove it themselves, so I said to the driver, " In three minutes, I'm going to be on that locomotive leaving for Chicago, whether your car is on the track or not." Having said that, I turned and started walking toward the engine. Of course I wouldn't have intentionally run into their car but they didn't know that. Anyway it worked, for in less than three minutes they were off the crossing and gone.

Freddy

In the mid to late sixties I was driving back and forth to Muncie, Indiana working a yard job. There was a switchman working on the job named Freddy who was medium height, built like a Mac Truck, and had a low raspy voice. One day, a few years earlier, while in a tavern near our railroad yard in Chicago, one of the railroaders became upset with Freddy and sucker punched him. In his low voice he said to the railroader, "Boy, if you can't hit any harder than that, you better get back on that bar stool and keep quiet." If Freddy had hit him, he would have knocked him into the middle of next week. . Freddy ordinarily drove an older car, but on this particular day, he showed up at work in a new Ford Tudor Sedan. Freddy was proud of his new car and took pride in pointing out all it's new features and changes to us. I was impressed with the new paint scheme, the redesigned grillwork and etc. As we were working the afternoon shift, we got off work between 11:00 and 11:45 pm. That evening, I started home in my 1953 Chevy that I used for a work car at that time. There is a road between Muncie and Marion called the Wheeling Pike. It was not the quickest way for me to go home for it was very narrow and crooked. but it was the shortest and sometimes I would go this way for a change of scenery. I had just left the city of Muncie and was going up through the country on this highway, when in my rear view mirror, I saw the grill work of Freddy's new car right on my tail. I knew my Chevy didn't stand a chance against Freddy's new car, but with me driving this road every few days, I knew that I knew the road better than Freddy, so I might be able to give him a pretty good run. The race was on. The Chevy, wide open would only do about 85, but with all the curves there weren't many places you could reach that anyway. Freddy hung right on my bumper. Farther down the road, we came up behind some traffic that I finally managed to get around. It wasn't long until Freddy got around the traffic and was right back on my bumper again. About this time I heard a siren and a red light came on, on top of Freddy's car, I sure didn't remember anything about a red light being on the top of it. In a situation like this, the best thing to do is stop. I did and the Ford pulled in behind me and stopped also. I waited in the car for whatever was about to develop. At this time I figured it was more or less out of my hands. I waited for what seemed like a long time, while the siren kept blowing and the red light kept flashing. Finally I got out of the car and walked back. I could see it was a sheriff's car and the sheriff was standing up in the driver's door way jamming, what looked like book matches, into the siren. I asked, "What are you doing?" He said, "I'm trying to get this siren to shut off." He finally got it stopped and asked to see my driver's license. He asked, "Where were you going?" I said, " I was trying to get away from you. You were following me so closely, I was afraid you were going to cause us both to wreck." He said, "I'm on call and I couldn't get around you." I said, "Well I don't know about that, but you had me pretty scared." He then handed me my license back and said," I've got to go-take it a little easier." He then got in his car and left. When I told Freddy the next day what had happened, we both had a big laugh.

Unexplained

While working at Muncie, we had to take a cut of cars up to Drew passing siding, just west of downtown Muncie, with the yard engine for an eastbound freight to pick up. We set the cars off and waited for the freight to pass and then we would follow him back to the yard. After waiting a very long time, we finally got the signal. When we returned, I saw a semi that had been demolished, sitting near the tracks. When the eastbound train had been approaching the downtown crossing, the traffic had become stalled with the semi on the crossing. Though the driver was warned the train was coming, he remained in the cab and was killed instantly. A lot of unexplained things like this would happen in connection with crossing accidents.

Buying The Chief

Though I hadn't flown an airplane since March 3, 1946, I still loved airplanes, and on occasion, would spend time at the local airport watching planes take off and land. While at this airport in 1965, I saw an airplane that really caught my eye. I had been offered a chance to buy one, identical to this one, nine years earlier when I lived in Alexandra, Virginia. I might also add it would have been seven hundred dollars cheaper at that time however; due to lack of funds, it was out of the question. The plane was an Aronica Chief, yellow with blue trim. No navigation equipment except a compass, top speed was ninety- two miles per hour. It had two seats and the engine was hand cranked. To me it looked like a million bucks and I just had to have it. I would have been back into flying sooner but with going to college, getting married, building a house and raising a family, money had become a scarce item around the household. I have many good memories with the Chief. Some were rather exciting. In the winter of 1967, I had wanted to do some cross-country flying. I was working pretty regular at the time and it seemed everyday I was in, the weather was always bad. After several weeks had gone by without good flying weather, on February24, 1967, I awoke to find a sunny day without a cloud in sight. I called the forecaster to get a weather briefing and he said, " In three hours, there will be snow in Central Indiana." I could not believe this. (Maybe I didn't want to believe it.) So to the airport I went, cranked up the Chief, and took off for Anderson, Indiana, in a beautiful sunlit sky. As the Chief didn't have any radio or navigation equipment, except the compass, navigation was strictly by pilotage. When I started to leave Anderson, I glanced toward the western sky, as that would be the direction I would be going to Frankfort, Indiana, my next stop. The sky was beginning to look pretty dark in that direction. However, if it got too bad, I could always turn back to Anderson. When I was approximately ten miles from Frankfort, I ran into light snow. In spite of the snow, the visibility still wasn't too bad. I looked at the aerial map and I could see a railroad track running below me that went right by the airport I was looking for, so I decided to follow it into Frankfort. As the airport came into sight, the snow got much heavier so I knew I had to get down as quickly as possible. As I landed and pulled up in front of the gas pumps, it really started coming down. Just as I got out of the plane, the attendant came out and said, "Man, how did you ever find this place?" I said, "Believe me, it wasn't easy." Leaving the plane there, due to the weather, I got a ride out to highway 31 and then caught a ride with a semi going to Peru. By this time the snow was getting deep and the highway slick. By the time we got to Peru, we had jacked knifed twice. I almost wished I were still in the airplane.

The Chief did make one emergency landing during the five and one half years I owned it. This happened on January 9, 1967. I had previously flown it to a private grass strip where an aviation mechanic had a shop to have the engine overhauled. After paying the mechanic, I started the plane to fly it home. Something about the engine sounded differently. I didn't know for sure if it was the engine or my imagination. But not being satisfied, I shut the engine down and ask the mechanic to come out and listen to it. He said he couldn't hear anything, but if I wanted, he would fly it around the field. I said, "OK, I'll go with you. "We taxied to the end of the runway and took off towards the west. The engine at full power sounded normal. However, when we reached approximately five hundred feet, there was a loud bang. It sounded as if a piston had come out through the side of the engine. He shut the engine down and we started looking

Aronica Chief and I somewhere over the Peru area.

The Chief and I at Weed Field.

Flying over Peru Yards along the banks of
the Wabash.

Night Run on a General motors locomotive.

When Things Go Wrong On The Railroad.

for a place to set down. Just ahead and to the left was a cornfield where the corn had already been cut so that's where we landed. When we got out, not knowing what we would find, we were somewhat relieved that it was only the spinner on the propeller that had come loose. We took the spinner off and the mechanic, who was a pilot, flew it out. A passer by who had stopped, after seeing us go down, gave me a ride back to the strip.

Rescue

During the summer of 1968, my wife and I along with our two sons, decided to go to the lake to water ski. After being there for some time, we had just passed under a bridge that crossed the lake at a height of about 120 feet. My wife had been running the boat and for some reason, I do not remember, had stopped. We were sitting in the boat approximately 300 feet east of the bridge when we heard what sounded like a shotgun blast. As I looked in the direction of the noise, I saw a column of water about ten feet tall in the air below the bridge. We tried to decide what had happened. Had something fell off the bridge? Had somebody fell off the bridge? Or had someone been shot and thrown off the bridge? I told my wife to start the boat and go over to where we had seen the water column. At first she refused, as she was afraid it might have been a shot and someone might be on the bridge with a gun. I told her we would have to take that chance as someone might be drowning. The water was very clear and as we neared the area, I could see a body in the water. He was in an upright position, leaning at about a forty- five-degree angle, with his head a couple of inches under the water. When I leaned down and grabbed him under the arms, I could feel the body was stiff so I thought he must be dead. As I attempted to pull him in the boat, the stiffness went away. His skin was a deep purple. He was a big man and though I tried, I just couldn't get him in the boat so I told my oldest son, who was about twelve years old, to help me and finally we got him aboard. He wasn't breathing but I didn't see any gunshots so I started giving him artificial respiration, as my wife got the boat turned around and headed for the marina. Just before we arrived at the marina, he started breathing and making noises. The emergency vehicle soon arrived and took him to the hospital. I later called the hospital to see how he was doing, and they said he was o k. I also heard that due to some bad business dealings, he had tried to commit suicide by jumping off the bridge.

The Fox

While we were still running the F-7s, as we reached the bottom of Okeann Hill, there was a light tan fox that would come up on the right of way and run along side of the engine like a dog will do with a car. It seemed to be a sport with him. Sooner or later it was bound to happen and one night when he tried to cross in front of the engine he didn't make it. We hated to see this happen, as he was a beautiful and unusual animal.

Bumpy Ride

One day a fellow engineer was working the west end yard job at Peru. On this job you would pull a cut of cars out on to a stub track that had a bumping post at the end of it. During his tour of duty, he was pulling a cut of cars toward the bumping post, and at the same time looking back for signals, from the switchman. He evidently he didn't realize how close he was to the end of the track or the sun was in his eyes, as he was headed west into the sun at the time. I don't know what time of day this happened but assuming it was afternoon this could have been the case. When he did see the bumping post, it was too late. The engine went through the bumping post and down an embankment that was just beyond it. The engineer didn't get hurt, but I suppose his ego might have suffered a little as I am sure he took a lot of ribbing over it.

1970s

Crash

On June 8, 1970, my birthday, I was called out of Chicago on First 98 at 4:30 am with units 2519, 6479, and 5871. During the trip home, one of the brakeman, who had half interest in a Cessna Sky Hawk, suggested that the four of us on the crew go flying in his airplane when we got in. Arriving at Peru at 1:19 pm, we headed for the airport. Before we boarded the airplane, I questioned the pilot as to the load we would be taking off with. He assured me we were within limits, as he had taken bigger loads than this off of this runway before. I suggested he take off with only two passengers, see how he got off, and then come back and pick up the other one. As I was the last one to get in, he said,   " Come on there's no problem." I figured it was his plane and he had been flying it for sometime so he ought to know what it would do. Soon after we left the runway, the stall warning went off. We couldn't lower the nose to gain speed as we were just above the treetops. At approximately 100 feet the plane began to loose altitude. The pilot found a vacant field and maneuvered as best he could toward it. Just before we touched down, the right wing stalled, dropped and dug into the ground. At this time, it swung around and the nose and left wing dug into the ground and we skidded to a stop. Soon after we got out the plane began to burn. We began putting dirt on the fire, but it didn't seem to help. We then started looking for and found a gas shut off. After that, we soon had the fire out. The pilot said the engine never did develop full power. Although there were some small injuries, I was glad we were able to walk away from it.

This was an unscheduled landing was bumpy also.

The Mooney

From the time I sold the Chief, August10, 1970, I rented planes to fly until October 1971, when two partners and myself, bought a four passenger Mooney. This was a more sophisticated airplane than the Chief. It had a constant speed prop, two radios, and retract gear. Its cruising speed was 140 mph (the Chief was a two passenger and cruised 92 mph.) Later two of us bought out the third partner and still later, I bought out the other partner. When my oldest son Michael, got back from Africa, after spending four years as a missionary, I taught him to fly the Mooney. He now has his own plane. In the nineteen years I owned this plane, it never missed a lick, except a couple times I unintentionally let it run out of fuel in one tank before switching to another. The Mooney had two main tanks in the wings and a reserve behind the back seat. The transfer valve was set to operate off anyone of the three tanks at a time. You would take off using one of the two wing tanks. After reaching cruising altitude (the altitude at which you intended to fly,) you would switch to the reserve tank. After it was depleted, you switched back to one of the wing tanks. When it was down to half, you switched to the other wing tank, depleted it, and then switched back to the first wing tank. If you calculated correctly, you would have enough fuel to take you to your destination plus forty-five minutes reserve. The first time I ran out of fuel before switching to another tank, my wife, my youngest son, my nephew, and myself were on our way to Daytona, Florida for a vacation. Directly over the city of Louisville, Kentucky, the engine coughed and I grabbed for the transfer valve, as I knew what had happened. My wife said, (what did you do that for,) as if I had planned it that way. Another time, I was in West Virginia over what used to be Lillybrook (a coal mining town of about 300 houses where we lived in the thirties) when the same thing happened. I had been sight seeing and had forgotten about the fuel being low in the tank I was using. A quick turn of the transfer valve brought everything back to normal. I'm sure glad it did for there was certainly no place for an emergency landing in that area. All that was in view were tree covered mountains and valleys. It took us eight to nine hours to drive to West Virginia. I could fly it in the Mooney in one hour and twenty minutes. I sold the Mooney June 24, 1991 and it was later totaled by someone in Missouri.

My son Gary and I in the Mooney.

Only By Inches

There are times when train and engine crews try to make moves while picking up or setting off, that will save time though it may not agree with company policy. This was one of those times. We had been called for the eastbound local out of Peru. We had orders on arrival at Phoenix to pick up a car out of the Dana Plant. The track ran easterly into the plant so we had to head in on it and this meant the car would be ahead of the engine and we would have to get it behind the engine. Company policy would have you cut off your train, pick up the car, pull it back and run around it in a yard track, pick the car back up, and shove it back on the train. When the brakeman asked me how we were going to do it? I said, We have only 40 empty cars, lets hang on to them, pick up the car, shove the train back the main line and as we do, drop the pick up and let it roll by us after the engine clears the yard track. Then we will pick it up and shove it on the train." The brakeman said, "ok." Everything was going well, as the brakeman, riding the pickup car, pulled the pin. I then pulled back on the throttle to speed up and give the brakeman time to throw the switch that would permit the car to roll by us. When the engine was about halfway through the switch, the brakes went into emergency. Luckily I had enough speed built up that our momentum carried us into the clear of the oncoming pick up car. Later we learned, the flagman riding the caboose whose eyesight was terrible, (how he passed his physical, I'll never know,) couldn't see the signal at the west end of the track. So thinking we were about to run passed the signal, he dumped the air. Though making the move the way we did saved us about twenty minutes, it almost came to naught, as the dropped car missed us only by inches.

Hobos

Train crews receive their clearances on a written form that permits you to occupy a specific section of track. Orders from the dispatcher are sent through the operator, who at this time was located in depots, towers, and operator shanties along the railroad. The operators would pass the orders to the crews by attaching them to an order hoop, that was equipped with a long handle that he could reach up to the crewman as the train went by or he could place the order hoop in a stand where it could be reached by the crewman as he passed by. As this was sometimes done at maximum speed, the string that held the orders on the hoop itself wound break. The train would have to be stopped and the brakeman would have to walk back and get the orders. On one occasion on an east bound freight, as we went by the depot at Lacrosse, Indiana, I got my orders from the hoop. When the caboose went by the depot the conductor called on the radio and said he saw a yellow order signal displayed (signifying there should have been orders in the hoop) however, there were no orders there. Rather than stop the train, I read my orders to him on the engine radio. As we reached the next eastward station, I saw the yellow order board displayed again. As I reached for my orders from the hoop, I turned and looked back, I suppose to be sure there were orders in the lower hoop for the rear end crew. Just as the first boxcar of the train went by the hoop, I saw an arm come out of the boxcar door and grab the orders. I hated to mess up the hobo's day, whom I'm sure was having a ball, but sometimes you got to do what you got to do, so I called ahead to the next station and had a welcoming committee of one, the Sheriff, waiting to greet him on arrival.

Broken Arm

While on a ski trip to Swiss Valley ski slope, in Michigan. I was resting at the top of a slope when my two sons came up to me and said, "Come on dad, have we found the place for you." I started following them to the slope they were speaking of. As I rounded a building, there was a steep down grade covered with ice. Before I knew what was happening, my skies went straight up, and I landed on one arm breaking it in two places. After going to the hospital in Three Rivers, Michigan and getting patched up; my skiing was over for the day. Of course, I don't know for sure, but I don't think this was what the boys had in mind. At this time, I had been working a road job. Though I knew I wouldn't be able to work that job, I thought as long as the company didn't know I had a broken arm, I could work a yard job. On a yard job, about all the work of running an engine is done with the right hand and it was my left hand that was broken. Also, since it was in the dead of winter, I would have on a big coat and no one would see the cast on my arm. A short time later it was time for the annual C&O Christmas Dance and Dinner. This was an annual event no one wanted to miss, including me for the dinner was fantastic, there were nice door prizes and all always had a good time. I knew there would be several company officials there and if they saw my cast, I would be pulled out of service until the cast came off. I was willing to take that chance but what I didn't know was that one of the officials would be sitting at my table. I kept my left hand under the table and the cast out of sight as much as possible. I don't know if he saw it, but if he did he didn't say anything. Maybe he understood my situation. That was another reason I enjoyed working for the C&O, we usually always had good officials to work for.

Mayhem

As I have said before, sometimes things happen on the railroad that's not funny at the time, but seems a bit more humorous when you look back. I was called out of Peru one morning on an eastbound local. Among our orders was an order to pick up a load of farm machinery off of an elevator track just east of Muncie. It had previously been on an eastbound when the load shifted. They had set the car out in the elevator track and had sent a crew down from Peru, approximately sixty- five miles away, to make the load secure once more. When we arrived at the elevator track, the brakeman cut the train off back of the signal to leave enough room to get the engine, and the car we were picking up, back of the signal. (You had to do this, as you had to have a signal, other than "all red" in order to leave. Without clearing the signal, and being behind it, the dispatcher couldn't give you a signal except an "all red" indication. We then ran the engine on the elevator track, which was a pretty steep up grade, to get the car. The idea was to get the car moving, cut away from it with the engine, run the engine back to the main line, over the switch, throw the switch, and then pull the engine far enough ahead of the train for the car to clear it when it came out of the elevator track onto the train. Then we would back the engine onto the train and be ready to go. This made our pick up car the first car in the train. The brakeman was supposed to ride the car out of the elevator track and set the hand brake to slow it down before coupling into the train. As I watched it come down the grade, I could see something was amiss. The car was running much too fast and about that time the brakeman jumped off. The car continued on, slowing down little if any, and slammed into the train. The wood bracing and steel bands that were holding the load broke loose again letting the load shift once more. All we could do was set the load out again, call Peru and tell them to send the repair crew back to re secure the load. The hand brake on the car was defective causing the collision.

Sun kinks And Derailments

Sometime early in the sixties or seventies, the railroad began to replace lengths of rail that were about eighty feet long and joined with tie bars, with "ribbon rail." Ribbon rail was continuous rail that had been welded together at the joints, rather than tied together with tie bars. This gave a much smoother ride, and it eliminated the click ah de clacks of the rail joints as you passed over them. However there was a down side to ribbon rail. It was affected by sever temperature change and in Indiana you get a lot of that. When you had a pronounced temperature drop, the rail would contract and would sometimes cause a "pull apart" at the rail joints. When the temperature would raise considerable, in a short length of time, it would cause "sun Kinks," (the rail would buckle due to expansion.) If the kinks were not too severe, you could pull your train over it at two to five miles per hour. High speed over a kink would usually spell disaster, as the train would off times derail. We were on an eastbound with a load of empty coal hoppers. Coming out of Lacrosse, Indiana on a hot summer afternoon, we could see something didn't look right on the rail up ahead. As it was so hot that day, we had been on the lookout for sun kinks. I slowed the train down in case we had to stop. Sure enough it was a serious kink. However we were able to move over it at two miles per hour. It was either that or wait for a track crew to come out and fix it, and it was any body's guess as to how long that would take. The Track Foreman was usually a little conservative and sometimes would not let you pass over a kink that an engineer would have attempted had the foreman not been there. Their being conservative was understandable for if he O ked the track and the train derailed, he would be held responsible. So if I thought I could make it, I always tried it before the foreman arrived for then it would be his decision.

I did have a derailment of an engine at Lacrosse one time. That was due to a yard track rail turning over in a curve. We were picking up cars there and were only moving about five miles per hour at the time. The lead unit dropped down rupturing the fuel tank on the rail and spilling about 3000 gallons of fuel.

Pulling a westbound out of Cincinnati one day in the early afternoon, we had just left the yard and had not yet gotten up to speed. We were doing approximately 35 miles per hour at the time. I looked back to check my train over, and as I did, I could see dust and ballast flying out from under a car approximately ten cars back of the engine. The car was just passing over an overhead bridge that crossed a highway there. I stopped as soon as I could. The car had remained upright fortunately until we were stopped. Had it overturned, the cars would have spilled down on the highway below and could have caused a very serious accident.

I was never involved in a very serious derailment. This I suppose was due mostly to luck and partially to always checking the train frequently on curves for defects. We would look for sparks from dragging equipment, smoke from overheated journals, (where the axels joined the undercarriage of the car,) or anything about the train that didn't look normal.

Coffee Bottle

I lived approximately five miles from the railroad yard. When called in the night, I had to get dressed, eat, drive to the yard, and be there in time to read and sign the bulletin books, and also see that the engines were checked over and ready to go. This had to be done in one hour from the time I received the call. One night in the rush, I forgot my coffee bottle. (It is common knowledge that an engineer cannot operate without a bottle of coffee). When I reached the yard, I called my wife and told her to take the bottle over to the crossing (about a quarter mile from my house) and set it on the electrical box there at the crossing. I had the train slowed down to about walking speed. The fireman jumped off, grabbed the bottle, and was back on in a minute or less. I don't remember if there was a car sitting there at the crossing at the time, but I'll bet if there was, he was wondering what was going on.

Tar Truck

Passing through downtown Muncie, Indiana, we went around a blind left-handed curve just west of a heavily traveled crossing. There was a tall building just to the left of the tracks and due to this tall building you could not see the crossing until you were about two or three car lengths from it. One night while going around this curve with a through freight out of Peru, Indiana for Cincinnati, I saw the head end of a semi truck come into view as it started across the crossing. In about one second, the front end of the tank he was pulling came into view. (This was a tank, as in gasoline tank truck.) Already, I was too close to stop and it looked as if we would hit him before he got a chance to clear. In the next instance, the filler cap on top of the tank came into view and I could see from the spillage around the cap, that it was a tank used for hauling tar instead of gasoline. He did clear but only by a few feet. Ordinarily, standard reaction would be to put the brakes in emergency, when I thought the truck might not clear, but with a gasoline truck, you don't want to stop a train with a gasoline truck hanging on the front end of your engine for you would be in the middle of a ball of fire. A better idea, when hitting a gas or gasoline truck was to hit them at full speed and hope you would knock them to one side or the other side of the track and then continue until you were out of the fire area before stopping. Usually a direct hit on one of these trucks would burn out the first and second units. An engine crew from another railroad, who stayed at our hotel in Chicago, hit a gas truck and both the fireman and engineer lost their lives. Three things an engine crew did not want to see on a crossing; a gas truck, a gasoline truck, and a loaded school bus.

All In A Days Work

While westbound on the local (a train that picks up and sets off cars where ever requested along the line) we had lost one of our locomotives, due to mechanical failure and the other one was about to run out of water. I stopped at a house near the track and went to the door. When a lady opened the door, I told her about my situation and ask if she had a hose I could run to the engine to fill it with water. She said, "No, but I got a bucket." I would have been there the rest of the day trying to fill that engine with a bucket.

While taking a manifest through Hammond, Indiana, just on the outskirts of Chicago, I was running only 10 miles per hour, the speed limit for trains through the area at that time. As I approached one of the many crossings, protected by lighted crossing gates, an auto struck my lead unit. At this speed I was able to stop in just a few feet. After determining no one was hurt, I asked the lady driving the car, for necessary information, such as name, address, license number and so forth. I ask her why she had driven through the crossing gates? She said she wasn't sure. As I thought she would want to know how much damage was done to the engine, I checked it over and told her the engine was ok as there hadn't been any damage to it. She replied, " I don't care about your damned old engine, look what you've done to my car."

You would not believe how much wild game there is around railroad yards, even in big cities like Chicago. The grain that spills out of grain cars attracts them. As we sometimes did our own cooking at the dormitory where we were staying while working yard and transfer jobs there. It was not unusual to have a rabbit or Ring neck Pheasant cooking in the pot. One morning when getting off work, I was walking across the tracks when I saw a railroad detective. Not wanting to explain why I was carrying two dead Ring neck Pheasants in the city limits, and Lord help me if he ask how I got them. I quickly put them under a car parked nearby and continued on until he was out of sight. Later I went back and got them. I thought I had pulled it off until he came by later and ask, " Jack, what time will the pheasants be ready to eat?

Blocking crossings around Chicago unnecessarily was a no, no as the cops got a little testy. One day as I was eastbound going by Burnham, the dispatcher took the signal from me so I stopped as soon as possible. However, I had already tripped the circuit that made the gates come down on a very busy crossing. I could not back up, as I did not have radio contact with the caboose. After sitting there for several minutes; waiting to get the signal, another train pulled up on the track to my right and went on down a little closer to the crossing. When he got near the crossing, a cop stopped him and started writing him a ticket as he thought this guy was the one who had caused the gates to be down so long. At this time I got the signal and started leaving town. As I went by, the cop was writing the ticket and the engineer, on the other train, was pointing at me while trying to explain to the cop it was I, not him, who had been blocking the crossing. Win some loose some. On another occasion, when I had blocked a crossing for sometime by being on the circuit and causing the gates to come down, another train pulled by me, and as he approached the crossing, an irate motorist began throwing rocks at him. I thought it was rather humorous, but I'm sure the other engineer didn't.

Saboteurs

On June 2, 1972, I was called for 2nd 98 out of Peru for Cincinnati. When we received our orders, this order was among them. (Run cautiously from the Indiana state line to Okeana, Ohio looking for saboteurs or track destruction.) Information had been given to the railroad that a conversation overheard in the Dayton, Ohio area, said the bridge, on Okeana Hill, would be sabotaged. I approached the bridge with quite a bit of apprehension, for this was a long, heavy train on a steep hill, and when we rounded the last curve before the bridge, we would be only a short distance from the bridge that was about one hundred and fifty feet high. I had to have the train under control and be able to stop short of the bridge or I would have to contend with a possible drop of 150 feet into the ravine. As I rounded the last curve, I was pleasantly surprised and relieved, for the whole valley was alive with police cars. A saboteur could not have gotten within a half mile of that bridge.

Oshkosh

On August 4, 1972, my two sons, Michael 16, Gary 12 and I, departed Peru in my plane, along with two other planes, for the Experimental Aircraft Fly In at Oshkosh, Wisconsin. We had food and camping gear with us, as we intended to camp out and sleep under the planes in our sleeping bags as my friends and I had done before. This was the first time I had taken my sons on this trip, and they were very excited. We had to pass over a portion of Lake Michigan en route. While we were out over the lake, at approximately 8500 feet elevation, I looked back toward the baggage compartment and saw a bag of potato chips that was tight as a drum. High elevation had caused it to expand. I wonder, if we had gone much higher and the bag would have exploded, throwing chips all over the cabin, how much excitement that would have added to the trip, to say nothing of the loud bang that would have gone along with it. Even seasoned travelers don't appreciate loud bangs in airplanes out over Lake Michigan. To anyone interested in flying, a trip to Oshkosh is a must. It is indeed the Granddaddy of all fly ins. I have never seen such a concentration of aircraft as is there. That night we had a summer night storm complete with thunder and lightening. The storm came as no surprise to us as we had experienced them on previous trips to Oshkosh. We had visqueen (plastic sheeting) draped over the wings so we managed to stay dry. The next afternoon, as we prepared to leave, we got in an unending line of airplanes, waiting to take off. There was a Traffic Director on the runway with signal paddles, like the ones used to give instructions to pilots on carriers. Every few minutes he would signal the next airplane in line to start its take off roll. To be in the air with so many aircraft was quite an experience. I had the good fortune of meeting and talking to "Chuck Yeager," the first pilot to fly faster than sound. Since he was also from West Virginia, I said, "Chuck, I guess you are about the only one from West Virginia that ever really amounted to anything." He laughed and said, "Oh, I don't know about that." He is a very likeable and friendly guy. I also got to talk to Bob Hoover, famous acrobatic pilot and flying buddy of Yeager's during the war. Also saw "Pappy" Boyington, leader of the "Black Sheep Squadron" in World War Two. We arrived back in Peru early that evening and the next morning, August 6, 1972, with my wife and two sons, departed on a flying vacation to Texas. At Evansville, Indiana the weather deteriorated, so after a short delay, we were off to Vicksburg, Mississippi. After spending the day in Vicksburg, sightseeing Civil War battlegrounds and museums, we left for Lake Charles, Louisiana. We soon ran into a lot of overcast. I said, " We should climb up over the cloud layer." My wife, not having done much cross -country flying said, "No, I don't want to do that." She didn't know about those alligators that were waiting for us in the swamps we were flying over, or the Indians who would strip a plane in nothing flat if it went down in that area. Finally the clouds got so low, I had to go on top and once up there, she thought the scenery was beautiful. At our next stop in Galveston, Texas, we landed at an airport along the coast and went for a swim in the warm waters of the gulf. San Antonio was our next stop. We rented a car and went sight seeing. In the early afternoon, we arrived in Austin, just ahead of some serious storms so we decided to spend the night there. The next morning, we took off for Arlington, Texas, to visit my wife's brother and his wife. On the way to Arlington, we picked up a tail wind and averaged 178 mph. that's pretty good for a plane that has a cruise speed of 140 mph. After a few days, we departed for Indiana. Over the mountains of Arkansas, both radios quit. I had the same trouble before we left. When I checked it out then, the mechanic had said the antenna cable had come loose. Since both radios quit at the same time again, I figured it had to be the same problem. At this time we were flying under a low cloud layer and over mountain ridges with no communication or navigation radios. I found Fort Smith, Arkansas on the aerial map and headed for it .As we crossed the last mountain ridge, I began getting a faint reading on my navigation radio. We landed and I asked the mechanic if he would check my radio antenna cable? Sure enough it was the same problem. I'll never forget he only charged me $3.50 to fix it. After a stop in Harrison, Arkansas, for fuel and lunch, we flew on to St Louis where we spent the night. Just pass noon on the 15th we were back in Peru. We had traveled 2300 miles in 21 hours flying time and had seen a lot of scenery.

Panic Time

While working on the Wabash Sub Division, (Peru to Chicago), during the summer of 1973, I was called for a westbound freight in the afternoon. After reaching a speed of 45 mph, we tipped over a hill where I could see approximately a mile ahead. I could see something on the track, but couldn't make out what it was. As we got closer, I could see men on the track. I started blowing the horn. We could see from their reaction that only then did they know that a train was coming. By now I had made out what appeared to be some type of machine on the track. The men began to work frantically as if they were trying to get the machine off the track. As we got closer, the men began to run. I had already put the brakes in emergency. However, I was sure we would not get stopped short of the machine. At this time, one of the men returned and again was trying to get the machine off. I had no idea what was going to happen when we hit the machine. We might knock it off the track or it might derail the engine and if that were the case, we would probably turn over in the ditch alongside the track. To make matters worse, there were approximately one hundred freight cars behind us in our train. Most of them were loaded and some of them might come in on top of us, as sometimes happens in train wrecks. I started blowing the horn again, as we were getting entirely too close for that man to be on the track. He finally ran, leaving the machine and we prepared for whatever was going to happen. When we hit the machine, there was a tremendous noise and impact, but we did stay on the rails. When the train stopped, we went back to talk to the men. They told us the regular Foreman was off and the substitute foreman had forgotten to notify the dispatcher, they would be working on the track at that location. The machine we hit was a new drilling machine, used to drill boltholes in the rails, and today was it's first day to be used. Though the machine had been attached to both rails, it had done very little damage to the locomotive. Only very small pieces were left of the machine. The foreman was a nervous wreck. He said," I just know they are going to fire me. " But I doubt they did for an experienced track man was hard to find.

Man On The Track

Coming out of Cincinnati for Peru, on a westbound freight, we had just passed downtown and were climbing the hill out of Richmond, Indiana. It was a nice sunny, summer day, approximately 3:00 pm. As we rounded the curve, I saw a man sitting on the end of a tie on the south side of the rail. Knowing we would not clear him, I began blowing the horn. When he didn't move, I immediately put the brakes in emergency. However we were much too close to stop in time. When the engine struck him, we were going about 20 miles per hour. He went flying through the air into the ditch alongside the track. Lucky for this guy, we had an F-7 with a rounded front end that threw him away from the train. On other type engines with the square front end, he would have been killed on impact or thrown under the train. As it turned out, I could tell from all the profanity he was using, he was very much alive. Seems as though he had too many drinks and decided to take a nap. With a little forethought he might have found a safer place.

Deep River

How Deep River ever got its name I'll never know. Approaching Deep River, you would go down a long descending grade, through a valley, at the bottom of which was a short bridge over a narrow creek and then up an ascending grade on the other side. One night on a coal train of 100 to 120 cars, we had just crossed the bridge, running 40 miles per hour, when I saw a piece of the ball of the rail, on the right hand rail was missing. It looked as if approximately six inches were missing. It was too late to stop and I hesitated dumping the air, as the train was on a downgrade, the slack would probably run in causing a derailment for sure. Instead I pulled a couple notches of throttle and drew off a little air to stretch the train and started slowing it down. I called the caboose and told them to brace themselves in case we didn't make it over. We did make it over and I called the operator at Griffith to report the track condition, estimating six inches missing. As we came through Griffith the next day on the return trip, the operator called me on the engine radio and said it had actually been eight inches of the top of the rail missing.

Stock Truck

Sometime in the early seventies, as I best remember, we were traveling westbound on a manifest freight, and we were passing through a 40-mile an hour speed restriction. We were approaching a curve around midnight when I saw someone standing by the track frantically waving his arms. I applied the brakes immediately, for down around this curve, and into a small community of Williamsburg, was all down hill. As we rounded the curve, I could see a semi trailer stock truck sitting on the crossing. We were able to get stopped short of the crossing. The trailer, which was very long, did not have enough ground clearance, and had hung up on the rail. If we had not received the signal in time to stop short of the crossing, the semi, the stock, and possible us would have been history.

My wife took this picture, from the car, at a crossing near our home. This would be one of my last runs from Peru to Cincinnati over the old Chicago Division prior to our terminal being moved to Chicago.

Let's Stay And Watch The Show

One afternoon my wife and I took off from the grass strip where I kept my plane hangared. We had made plans earlier to pick up another couple at the local city airport and then fly to Rochester, Indiana for dinner. It was beautiful with sun shining brightly and very little wind. The city airport was just a short distance away, so they were soon in the plane and we were on our way. Enroute to Rochester, we passed over Lake Manitou, just on the south side of Rochester. Years ago, before the Mississinewa Reservoir was built near our home; we used to go water skiing and boating on this lake. On a winter's day a few years earlier, during ice fishing season, I flew over this lake and saw seven cars and one truck all parked together on this lake. I still don't understand how the ice held all that weight or why those guys would have put the ice to a test this severe. After dinner we returned to the Peru airport. When I stopped to let the couple out of the plane, I saw a friend of mine taxiing out to take off in an "Ultra light" aircraft. Ultra lights are usually home built from kits. In most cases, they are capable of hauling light loads only, as they are powered with small engines. My friend, being a big man, I wondered how well he would get off the runway. Especially since this was a very hot day and temperature plays a big roll in how an aircraft performs. I turned to my friends and said, "Let's stay and watch the show." Little did I know! I shut my plane down; we got out and watched as he taxied to the south end of the runway. After what seemed a long time, he lifted off. The plane climbed slowly for about one hundred feet and then the nose dropped. Then it came back up only to drop again. By now it was quite obvious he was in trouble. For the third time the plane descended and disappeared behind a big stand of evergreen trees at the northwest end of the runway. At this time we heard what sounded like a plane crashing through tree limbs. I started running in the direction where he disappeared. I ran through the trees and never saw anything. I then started through an adjoining cornfield. By this time I could smell gasoline, but didn't see any wreckage. Soon after, I heard voices. I made myself heard and ask if they had found him? They said yes, he had already been picked up. They had come in from the other side of the field with a truck. He was a little beat up, but the plane had gotten the worst of it. The noise we thought had been the plane crashing through the trees, had actually been the propeller hitting the cornstalks in the field. He had come down in behind the trees. This was the same friend, who was piloting the plane we had crashed in a few years before. His luck didn't improve with time for some four or five years later, as he was driving home from work, in the early morning hours, his vehicle left the road and plunged down an embankment. He died shortly thereafter and though we sometimes had our differences on the job, he was a very likeable, intelligent person whose company and friendship I enjoyed for years.

Miggs

My two sons and I decided to make a flying trip to Chicago to do some sight seeing the next day. That morning we awoke to a bright sunny day. I called weather for a pilot weather briefing, and we were soon on our way to the airport. After a preflight check of the airplane, we took off headed northwest for Chicago. As we crossed over the level, green fields of Indiana, we could see the outline of Lake Michigan in the distance. Many times, when flying through the clear skies of Indiana, as you approach the lake, you run into a lot of fog or haze, or a combination of both. Today, however, I could see it was severe clear. Flying northbound along the lake, you come to the high-rise buildings. This is, or was, the point where most pilots reported in when landing at Miggs. They were referred to as "The Hotels." I called in, "Mooney 23 Bravo approaching hotels, landing Miggs, request advisories." The controller came back on the radio with my landing instructions. Approaching Miggs, it resembles an aircraft carrier as it was built out in the lake. Landing and taking off there is quite an experience. Northbound takeoffs are right hand turnouts to avoid the tall buildings in downtown Chicago. After landing, we went to the Museum Of Science And Industry on Lake Shore Drive. After spending several hours there, we went to the aquarium that is close by. After going through the aquarium, we walked back to the airport and went up in the tower. As I talked to the Controller, a Cessna was landing and as it touched down, I said to the Controller, "It looks like that Cessna has a flat." At that moment, the pilot of the Cessna called in to report he had a flat. He was able to get the plane stopped without any serious damage.

We left the tower, went to the plane. did a preflight and called for a takeoff clearance. We were given the clearance with the standard right hand turn out for Miggs. The return trip, in a beautiful sunlit sky, was successful with a before sunset landing.

Hot Air Balloon

While working the west end yard job one cold winter night, we had worked up to about a half hour before quitting time at 7:59 AM. The Yardmaster had sent us to the Rip Track (an area, in the yard, where railroad cars were repaired.) It was very cold and frosty that morning and the river was frozen over. While working, I began to hear a very unusual noise coming from the direction of the river that ran parallel to the tracks. When I turned in that direction, a hot air balloon, approximately one hundred and fifty feet away, was descending toward the river, which at that time was frozen over. As I had never seen a balloon that low, within the city limits, I thought he might be in trouble. As I watched, he descended to within about two to three feet of the ice and then started to go back up. So evidently, he was just out for a joy ride.

Big Hook

An Engineer friend of mine was called for the "Big Hook." (A crane, used to rerail locomotives and railroad cars that have been derailed or overturned.) On the way to the wreck, where they were to use the "Big Hook,) they were going around a curve when the big hook overturned. Pulling speed of the big hook was usually ten to twenty miles per hour. I do not remember what was determined to be the cause of the derailment, broken rail, too much speed, burned off journal, etc. For whatever reason, it must have been somewhat depressing for the train and engine crews. I'm sure they never heard the last of it for quite a while. The crews always thought something like this was funny, if they were not at fault, but I'm sure the company looked at it from a different light.

Being Gone

I guess the toughest part of railroading for me was being gone away from home so much when I was low on the seniority list. The younger men had to work the out of town jobs and you miss seeing your kids grow up and watching them play sports. I remember I got in on a run late in the evening when my oldest son was playing football in a town approximately sixty miles away. I drove my old Chevy work car much faster than I should have trying to make the game. When I arrived, I found my son had just received an injury and was not able to play the rest of the game.

Cow

On a sunny day, about ten miles east of Peru, as we were approaching a railroad bridge, I saw what looked like an animal on it. I started blowing the horn and by now I could see it was a horse or cow. It stood up and tried to move, but one of its feet was stuck. Now I could see it was a cow. When I saw it was stuck, I tried to stop, but it was too late. As we got near, it laid down and as we passed over it, the usual noises, when hitting an animal, were heard. I expected the animal to be ground to pieces, as there is a very low clearance beneath the engine. However, when we got stopped and went back, the cow was dead, but still in one piece, except for one foot that was missing. It was probably the one that had been hung up. Though no other injuries could be seen, I'm sure the bruises and broken bones would have been enormous.

When a newly promoted Engineer ran a stop signal, causing
a collision with another train, it turned out to be a four million dollar
mistake.

Running Amtrak

On November16, 1974, I marked up on the Amtrak passenger run between Peru and Chicago. I was called for 11:25 AM the next morning with engine # 207 as the lead unit and # 204 as the second unit. We departed 12:07 PM, arrived 1:23 PM central time, and went off duty at 2:25 PM. We were on duty for four hours and I earned $54.71. Not bad for 1974, I guess. We took our train to, and left from Union Station, which is right down-town in the "Loop." We stayed in a hotel just a few blocks away called The LaSalle. What I didn't like about this job was the long layover. We would usually get in about 2:30 PM and wouldn't be called until about one or two PM the next day. On occasion, I would take my wife or one of my sons along, and we would have plenty of time to sight see, go shopping, visit museums and so forth. When I first took this job, we were going the old route into Chicago through Griffith, Indiana. Later, we started turning on the B&O line out of Lacrosse, Indiana and then on to Chicago on the B&O main line. When we ran the old line through Merrillville, Indiana about every trip, someone would blockade the track. Though I was running 50 to 55 mph, in that area, I wasn't too concerned as it was kid stuff-rocks, cans and etc. Later it got contin ously worse, such as ties being butted again other ties that were under the rails and pointed toward the engine. Being more concerned with this situation, I called the operator who notified the agent in that area.

While I was working Amtrak, my wife and I were returning from a vacation in West Virginia on Amtrak. I had called the crew caller in Peru before I left West Virginia and marked up on my job. Before arriving in Peru, I went to the diner to eat. The attendant on duty said " Sorry, you are too late, we are closed." I knew it was too early in the day for him to be closed so I said, "Well I am going to be your engineer from Peru to Chicago so you had better find some way to open it up." He said, "Yes sir, and what would you like? I worked this job until the following April when I was displaced by an engineer with more seniority. Later in 1974, I took Amtrak again also in 1975 and 1976. By this time it was a good job. We had new engines (700 series) and the layover was much shorter. I made my last trip on Amtrak December 1, 1977. We were called out of Chicago 9:25 Am-off duty, in Peru, 3:05 PM. The engine was a General Motors number722. I do not remember if I gave Amtrak up this time or if I was bumped off it.

When A Train And A Semi Met

Later on that same year, I was on an eastbound freight going to Cincinnati. As we approached a crossing in a little town of Williamsburg, Indiana, a semi truck, loaded with fence post, was also approaching the same crossing from the right. To the left of the crossing, was a grain elevator, and setting by the elevator were two loaded farm wagons. The two wagons were hooked to a farm tractor and were waiting to be unloaded. As the truck neared the crossing, he slowed down as if he was going to stop clear of the crossing, but instead he continued up on the crossing slowly and I knew he didn't have time to make it across. The head brakeman dove for the floor and the fireman lit on top of him. I started out the back door, thinking I would go to the second unit. However, as I started out the door, I realized I would not have enough time. I turned back and dove down behind the control stand. I haven't any idea how long it took to load that truck with fence post, but I know we unloaded it in about three seconds. When we got stopped and the dust had cleared away, we had missed the truck cab, hitting the trailer only. From the impact, the post had all came off and both post and trailer went into the farm wagons causing heavy damage to the farm wagons and scattering corn all over the nearby landscape. Before I could get off the engine, the farmer, who owned the tractor and farm wagons came up to the engine and asked, "Where is that truck driver? I'm going to kill him." He was one mad farmer and he looked big enough and mean enough to do it.

Confusion

When we were working out of Rockwell Street Yard in Chicago, the C&O had previously bought out the Pierre Marquette Railroad. This was a line running out of various cities in Michigan to Chicago. The crews of the PM, as it was called, also stayed at the same facility as the C&O crews. Though we knew some of the PM crews, most of them you knew only by sight and most of them not at all. This was also due to the fact that crews were always changing. You might see a guy one day and not see him again for a year or maybe never. There was not a twenty-four-hour restaurant in or near our dormitory where we stayed, so the company furnished a car for the crews to ride to a restaurant. Sometimes the car would be full of C&O crews, sometimes PM crews, or sometimes a mixture of both. On this particular day it was a mixture of both C&O and PM crews. They were on their way to a restaurant when a Chicago policeman stopped them. The policeman walked up to the car and told the driver he was going to give him a ticket for having a rear taillight out. The driver said, "This is not my car. The cop asked "Are you from Chicago?" The driver said, "No, I'm from Indiana." Then the cop asked one of the men in the back seat," Are you from Indiana." He said, "No, I'm from Michigan." The cop asked, "Where are you going?' One of them said, "We are going to a restaurant to eat." The policeman asked, "Which one of you does own the car?" None of us one of them answered it belongs to the company we work for. Cop says to driver, "What's your name?" Driver says," I'm not going to tell you, for if I do, you will give me a ticket and I told you the car does not belong to me." The cop asked the guy sitting behind the driver, what is this guy's name? He said, "I don't know." He then asked the guy in the middle of the back seat what the driver's name was. He said, "I don't know either." By this time the cop was getting a little bent out of shape. He asked the one he was talking to what's your name? He replied, " If he's not going to tell you his name, I'm not going to tell you mine either." The cop says," Now let me get this straight. I have a driver from Indiana, hauling passengers from Michigan, riding in a car with Illinois license plates, going to a restaurant to eat, with guys, who all work for the same company and none of you know each other? The driver says, That is right officer." The policeman threw up his hands and said, get that car out of here!

Unusual Event

During this time I was on the Engineers extra board. On the days I wasn't working and if I weren't doing something else, like going to the lake with my family, I would head for the airport. On the way, I would stop at the crew caller's office and check to get an idea of when I might be called to work. I had an agreement with the callers, if I got called, they would move the company truck they used from it's usual parking place to the other side of the track that ran by their office. I could see from the air if the truck had been moved and would know I had been called. On one of these bright sunny mornings, I saw on the board that one of my engineer buddies, Ralph Weideman, was getting out on a westbound freight soon. I went to the airport, got the plane ready, and took off. I flew northwest of town and climbed to about 2500 feet so I could see when his train left the railroad yard. After his train left town, I turned back toward him and dropped down over the track. As the distance between us closed, I pulled up over him. He still hasn't forgot about that.

He said "Jack, I can just see the newspaper headlines now. **Airplane And Train Have Head on Collision."** I guess that would have been a first or at least an unusual event.

Climbing The Ladder

You never knew what situation you might run into at the "Dog"(the company building where we stayed at Cheviot.) As I was leaving an upstairs sleeping area one day, I heard voices coming through a back window. I looked out the window and coming up the ladder was a brakeman and his girlfriend. He was holding on to the ladder with one hand and to a bottle with the other. I could tell from their conversation, they had already had more than enough to drink. I don't know what their intentions might have been, but women were strictly prohibited in the up stairs sleeping area.

Lucky Guy

Leaving Chicago on a freight train, we had just departed the yard when a train ahead of us stopped. After sitting there for a while, the flagman walked over from the caboose. When he got to the engine he said" Jack, don't move, there is a guy back there under one of our cars." We went back to take a look. He had been drinking, got under the car and passed out. After several attempts to remove him with no success, we called the yard and they sent a policeman out to remove him. Lucky for that guy, the brakeman decided to walk over to the head end or he would have been a goner.

Snowstorm

On a winter's night in the mid 70s my telephone rang. It was the crew caller telling me I was called for an eastbound grain train for Cincinnati. After turning on my driveway light, I could see it was snowing hard and drifting badly. I called him back and told him I didn't think I could make it into town but I would try. When I was only a city block from my house I knew it was impossible, so I turned in the first driveway to get off the highway. I walked back home, as there was no way I could get the van turned around without getting stuck. I called the railroad and told them I couldn't make it. The caller said I don't know what we are going to do as the train needed to be run and he could not find any available engineers. I told him if you can talk the fireman into bringing it to the top of the hill, which was about one quarter mile due east of my house, I will try to walk over and get on the train there. As Fireman Tschiniak agreed to this plan, we were soon under way. Once I got the speed of the train up, the snow and snow drifts were so high, all you could see was flying snow for five or six miles. At this point, the track turned more toward the east and the drifts were not so high. During this time, I had to blow the horn continuously to keep it from blowing full of snow and freezing up. I don't remember anymore about that trip, so evidently the situation must have improved.

Thunderstorm

In 1977, my wife and I decided to fly the Mooney to Kitty Hawk, North Carolina for a week vacation. We had invited another couple, Clyde and Betty Catin, to go along. Clyde was a shop foreman in the C&O mechanically department at Peru. I called the weather bureau early that morning for a weather briefing. They reported it being a little "iffy" but not impossible. At Hamilton, Ohio, just north of Cincinnati, we began picking up rain so we landed and waited for it to pass. Later we took off for Ashland, Kentucky to get fuel and to check on the weather, as it was getting extremely hazy. After we landed there, I called weather, gave them my intended route, and asked for a briefing. He told me the visibility would be very low but I would be able to "punch" through it. Though the sun was shining as we left Ashland, some hour or so later, the visibility began to deteriorate rapidly due to the haze. Somewhere over the mountains of West Virginia, between Ashland and Beckley, (I say somewhere because I didn't have any ground reference) we ran into the middle of a thunderstorm. The rain came down like it was being poured from a barrel. The plane suddenly began to ascend. As I glanced at my Climb and Descend indicator, it showed we were climbing at the rate of 1200 feet per minute. Soon afterwards, we stopped ascending, the radio mike left it's bracket, hit the ceiling, and fell to the floor. I picked it up and placed it back in its holder. At the same time the engine started to stall from fuel starvation due to the fuel being at the top of the tank. This was caused from going from ascending to descending so quickly. I glanced at the indicator and again it showed 1200 feet per minute, not that this was exactly our descending speed for that was as high as the instrument would register. After some time, we again reversed directions and started up again. By this time, I had reduced the power to slow flying speed and was concentrating on keeping the plane level as I didn't have any ground reference and I could not see beyond the wing tips. We reversed directions and started down the second time, now the engine was again at idle, and again the mike hit the ceiling, and then the floor, where it stayed for I was now too busy trying to keep the plane right side up. Though I had read articles that said when caught in situations such as this you should continue straight ahead. I just didn't think the Mooney could take much more of this, so I made a one hundred and eighty degree turn and soon we were out of it. We returned to Ashland and waited for the storm to pass. After we landed, the first thing I did was check for structural damage. Finding none, I understand how Mooney got the nickname of "Iron Sled". An hour or so later, the weather cleared and we were off. As we approached Beckley, West Virginia a wall of thunderheads and lightening streaks again blocked our intended flight path. After landing at Beckley and getting a weather briefing, which didn't show any improvement until late in the day, we left the plane there, rented a car and drove on to Kitty Hawk. When our stay on the beech at Kitty Hawk was over, we drove the car back to Beckley, picked up the plane and flew to Charleston, West Virginia to spend the night with our friends Carl and Lucille Bennett. The Charleston Airport (now called Yeager Airport) is located on top of a mountain. After we landed, I told the line boy to fill the main tanks only, as we had four passengers and our luggage. By filling the reserve tank also, we would have been overloaded. The next morning, when we arrived at the airport, I ask for my fuel bill. I could see there were far more gallons on the bill than my two main tanks would have held. When I checked the reserve tank, it had been filled also. I informed the office of the problem, and they readily agreed to drain the reserve. Later as we departed on runway 23, I was glad we did drain the reserve tank for at the end of the runway is about an 800 foot drop into the river valley. With an overloaded airplane, we would have probably become part of the scenery in the valley. After about two hours, in beautiful flying weather, we were back in Peru.

In the winter of 1978, I was eastbound on a merchandise train, when I ran into a blizzard. After being on the road for about three to four hours, the snow was getting pretty deep and the wind was picking up causing serious drifting in some locations. At Boston, Indiana we headed in a sidetrack to meet a westbound. After waiting about an hour for him, he finally went by. The dispatcher tried to throw the switch to let us out of the sidetrack, but due to the drifting snow he could not get the switch thrown over. The brakeman tried to clean the snow out, but it would blow back in before we could throw the switch. We finally gave up and called a track crew out of Cincinnati. From the time we arrived in the sidetrack, until we departed, five a one half hours had passed. Before we could make it to our destination terminal, due to the delay, our twelve- hour working limit had expired, and they had to send a crew to relieve us. I remember they picked us up in a van whose backseat heater had quit working, and we nearly froze before we got in.

Passing through Muncie, Indiana on an eastbound freight during the seventies, I   had just gone under a railroad underpass, across a city street, and had started through a second underpass when I felt the engine lurch. I turned quickly and looked back, thinking one of the other units might have derailed. Just as I went under the second underpass and before going around a curve, I had a glimpse of a red convertible with its rear end up against the second unit. It was plain to see he had rammed the second unit while going backwards. I ask the driver if he would please explain this unheard of proceeding, leading up to this collision. Many times I had one of my units run into, but never by a vehicle going backwards. He said, "Well, when I saw I wasn't going to make it over the crossing ahead of you, I hit my brakes, my left front brake grabbed, spun me around and I hit the engine going backwards.

As it turned out, it was probably the best move he could have made, as he didn't have any injuries.

In 1978 we started running over the B&O out of Cottage Grove, Indiana to Cincinnati. Going this route took us through the small towns of Hamilton and Glendale, Ohio. One misty, foggy night, as I approached the main crossing in Glendale, I saw a woman standing in the middle of the track just beyond the crossing. I had been blowing the horn as we approached the crossing, but due to mist and fog was unable to see her until we were very close. I reached for the train brake to dump the air, but just as I did, she jumped into the ditch alongside the track. I remember she was wearing a long, tan trench coat. I wondered what could have driven her to this and why she changed her mind?

Three Out Of Four

On this same crossing at Glendale, on another foggy night, we were approaching the crossing not running very fast due to restricted city speed limit when a big four-door car came up on the crossing. Everything, except the right rear corner cleared. When we hit him, it spun him around. We then struck him again, and then again, and a third time before he was knocked in the clear. By this time three of the four corners of his car had been demolished. I wonder how he explained this one to his wife?

The Willys

In the late 1970s I mentioned to my brother Dave, who lived on the outskirts of Cincinnati, I was looking for an old Jeep to restore. Ever since I had been in service I had wanted one, but never took the time to get serious about it. About two weeks later he called and said, "I found your Jeep." He told me it belonged to an old man who had used it to go fishing but due to poor health was no longer able to do so. I told him to buy it, and get fixed what ever it needed to get it ready to drive to Peru, about 150 mile away. When I went to pick it up, I do believe it was the most ugly vehicle I had ever seen. It was a faded out red color, with a homemade looking metal top and it still had the original sixteen- inch wheels. I drove it to the motel where we were staying on our layover runs to Cincinnati and parked it in the back of the parking lot. When my wife and I drove from Peru to get it, before we had even turned into the parking lot she saw it and said, "What did you buy that thing for?" After being restored, it was dark green, with a new convertible top, white wheels and new light brown leather seats. We have enjoyed driving it in several parades since then. Sometimes the grandkids have ridden with us. They think it's great and even my wife comes up for air when I mention that I might sell it. I guess that's out of the question anyway as my oldest son has already informed me that when I'm done with it, it belongs to him.

The author and his 1948 restored Willis jeep.

Topping the hill out of Peru for Cincinnati.

Small World

While I was running Amtrak I asked my oldest son, Michael, if he would like to go on a trip with me to Chicago. It was either during the summer, when he was out of school, or it was on Saturday, I don't remember. As there was a vacant seat on the engine, I let him ride in the cab with the fireman and I. The next day on the return trip, we came to the diamond at Griffith. This was where the C&O tracks crossed over the EJ&E tracks and also the Grand Trunk tracks. There was a fifteen- mile per hour slow order over this diamond and as we were crossing the diamond, I saw a man coming out of the C&O operator's shanty just beyond the diamond. This guy was wearing a white hard hat, like the ones some of the C&O officials would wear at times. As he walked toward the track, on which I was running he gave me a pick up sign that meant he wanted to get on the engine. I didn't know this fellow and thinking he might be an official, I told my son to go back and ride the rear unit so he wouldn't know he was on there for it was company policy that no one other than employees could ride the engine. This guy got on, introduced himself and said he was with the line and signal department and would like to ride to Peru with us. After we got home, we ate, my son took a shower and left. The next day he said, "Dad, I had a date with this girl last night. When I went to the door, I rang the door bell and you'll never guess who opened the door." I said, "No, I guess not-who was it?" He said, "It was her Dad, the guy that got on the engine at Griffith."

Passenger Trains

People who have never ridden a good passenger train such the C&O's George Washington that operated on the C&O mainline in the forties have really missed a lot. Beautiful scenery, plenty of room to relax, being able to get up, walk around, and go to the dining car for a good meal. When you got to where you were going, you were right downtown not fifteen miles out in the middle of nowhere at an airport looking for a rental car. Don' get me wrong. I feel as safe in a small plane, with the right pilot, as I do in a car, and I love flying in them. There have been a few times when I have been in a few tight places, but it wasn't anything I didn't manage to come through. When you get in trouble in a big plane you are really in trouble. I don't need that and neither do a lot of other people. If the government can subsidize airlines, and have for years, with our tax dollars, why can't they subsidize the passenger trains and let us taxpayers have a choice as to how we want to travel. The reason is the politician's travel on the airlines so that's where the subsidies go. You know there is some of us who are not in that big a hurry to get where we are going. We would rather take our time, enjoy the scenery, and relax. Unless there are some big changes in airline operation, it is my opinion that some day, we will have to return to train travel to relieve the congestion. I have never ridden on a Canadian train but I hear they are far superior to anything Amtrak has to offer.

The Day My Luck Ran Out

Up until the afternoon of May 8, 1978, when I was called for an Extra East at 3:20 PM, I had been very fortunate. Over the thirty years I had been employed by the C&O, I had never been involved in a crossing accident with fatalities. By 8:oo PM that day, I would no longer be able to say that. We left Peru with General Motors # 4048 as the lead unit and 4266 as the second unit. It was a warm sunny day. We stopped at Marion, Indiana to do some switching at the St Regis Plant, (an industrial plant we served,) and to pick up some cars. After we had done our work and coupled to the train, one of the trainmen realized they had made a mistake, so we had to cut off the train and go back in the industrial track to make the correction. The time we used in doing this would be very detrimental as to what would happen an hour or so later. Though I was working without a fireman, the head brakeman and the conductor were in the head unit with me. We were running about fifty mile per hour as we approached the west signal at Drew, just west of Muncie, Indiana. As we past the whistle post, located 800 feet from the crossing, I began blowing the horn and turned the bell on. As we got nearer the crossing, I saw a pick-up truck approaching the crossing from the east. I wasn't too concerned as he still had plenty of time to stop. I continued blowing the horn and though by this time he should have been slowing down, I could see he wasn't. I put the brakes in emergency and stood up in the cab where I could see the driver in the truck. At this time he locked up the brakes and started skidding toward the engine. I could see him very clearly through the trucks windshield. He was gripping the steering wheel with both hands as though he was applying great pressure on the foot brake. Though I could see there were others in the truck through my side vision, I did not know if they were men, women, or children, as I was concentrating on the driver. As near as I could determine, approximately one half of the truck was in front of the engine before the collision. On impact, the truck appears to explode and flew off to the left of the engine as we passed by. Never before had I witnessed an impact of this magnitude in a crossing accident. I knew, at this time, who ever was in that truck at best, would be seriously injured. By the time we got stopped, we were twenty to twenty five car lengths east of the crossing. As soon as the engine stopped, I started running back toward the crossing. I hated the thought of getting there, knowing what I was going to find, but at the same time thinking I might be able to help save someone's life. When I arrived at the scene, it had already been determined by those already there, that all three occupants were dead. There was a man and his two sons, ages 7 and 3. I went to a house nearby and ask the occupants if they heard my horn blowing. They verified that they did. I heard later, these same people had said they didn't hear it. It was quite obvious the accident could have been prevented. We measured the skid marks at 80 feet. If he couldn't have gotten stopped, he could have turned in either direction up or down the track alongside the train. No doubt it would have been a rough ride, but at least not life threatening. I did notice the sun was setting straight down the highway, so maybe he had been partially blinded by it. However, he should have heard the horn. I learned later, from one of the family members, if the driver's daughter had not decided to stay home and play with her neighbor friend, she too would have been in the truck. Though I had done everything I could to prevent this accident, I couldn't get the accident scene to go away. When it finally did, for along time it kept coming back. All crossing accidents are bad, but when kids are involved, they are much worse.

THE CHESAPEAKE AND OHIO RAILWAY COMPANY
WESTERN DIVISION
CINCINNATI-CHICAGO DISTRICT
SENIORITY ROSTER
ENGINEERS AND FIREMEN

JANUARY 1, 1983

NAME		ID NO.	EMPLOYED AS FIREMAN	PROMOTED TO ENGINEER
Cox	JJ	2267333	06-29-42 (01)	02-11-47 (01)
Wayne	EM @	2034036	11-12-42 (02)	- . - -
Wolfe	DE *	2278425	04-08-43 (03)	11-10-47 (02)
Longnecker	RC *	2052654	11-19-43 (04)	11-10-47 (03)
Kloenne	RE @	2032122	02-19-45 (05)	- - -
Hiers	DG	2031631	02-19-45 (06)	07-04-48 (04)
Denham	JJ	2030905	02-23-45 (07)	07-04-48 (05)
Dagnen	KG @	2030845	02-24-45 (08)	- - -
Randozzo	J	2086046	03-19-45 (09)	07-04-48 (06)
Hyde	NF	2023463	12-13-45 (10)	02-10-49 (07)
Scheuer	RR *	2000322	12-16-45 (11)	02-10-49 (08)
Woods	CR *	2027657	12-17-45 (12)	02-10-49 (09)
Grant	JC	2022592	12-21-45 (13)	02-10-49 (10)
McNary	RA	2024693	01-14-46 (14)	04-24-51 (11)
Behny	RE	2020373	01-14-47 (15)	04-19-62 (12)
Kuch	RC @	2023990	01-27-47 (16)	- - -
Leedy	RL	2024171	03-08-47 (17)	05-03-62 (13)
Pyeritz	NT	2025691	03-15-47 (18)	05-03-62 (14)
Cotcamp	O	2178855	08-28-47 (19)	07-02-62 (15)
Roll	HA	2025919	11-13-47 (20)	07-02-62 (16)
Langer	GA	2184297	11-27-47 (21)	07-03-62 (17)
Cakes	EL	2046041	12-31-47 (22)	01-03-63 (18)
Olinger	JRJF	2184115	01-06-48 (23)	01-03-63 (19)
Crosthwaite	JB	2182528	05-27-48 (24)	01-04-63 (20)
Young	JO	2027810	07-27-48 (25)	01-05-63 (21)
VanDyke	RB	2027176	07-31-48 (26)	01-12-63 (22)
Stevens	EB	2279388	08-03-48 (27)	4-19-63 (23)
Ivey	KL	2023531	08-29-48 (28)	07-02-63 (24)
Knox	WE *	2185489	10-08-48 (29)	07-02-63 (25)
Weideman	RG	2087171	04-01-56 (30)	07-12-63 (26)
Specht	JE @	2176625	04-01-56 (31)	- - -
Young	DL %	2146749	04-02-56 (32)	08-21-63 (27)
Cave	DA	2071553	04-03-56 (33)	08-25-63 (28)
Nance	RW	2185858	04-11-60 (34)	02-22-64 (29)
Hutchison	RN	2288487	04-25-60 (35)	02-23-63 (30)
Bowman	RC	2072806	07-15-60 (36)	07-17-64 (31)
Yoder	JL	2097049	08-16-61 (37)	07-17-64 (32)
Harvey	EL	2072997	11-18-61 (38)	07-17-64 (33)
Prior	JB	2280903	12-03-61 (39)	07-17-64 (34)
Pickering	ML	2087287	12-23-61 (40)	07-17-64 (35)

Mushrooms

Indiana "Hoosiers" takes great sport in wild mushroom hunting in the spring of the year, and railroaders are the most dedicated. Maybe it's because they always seem to grow so well along railroad tracks. I was called for a work- train east out of Peru early one spring morning. My fireman was Charlie Frazier, one of my favorites. Charlie, like me, was a displaced "Hillbilly". Though I was from West Virginia and he was from Kentucky, we were both from the same side of the river. He was an avid coffee drinker and before I could get whistled off, he was pouring me a cup of coffee. We always drank two thermos bottles each way on a trip. I let Charlie run the engine quite often so he would get the experience. By late afternoon we were still spreading balace. (This is stone used around and under ties to keep the moisture away.) During this operation you only move about 2 miles per hour with a lot of stops in between. While Charlie was running the engine, and since they were giving all the signals on his side, I decided to walk ahead and look for some mushrooms. Thinking Charlie knew I was getting off, I proceeded some 100 to 150 feet ahead. While canvassing the local terrain for those delicious morsels, I suddenly heard a "toot-toot" on the engine horn and at the same time, the engine began revving up very rapidly with black smoke pouring out the stacks. This told me two things, Charlie had gotten a highball (meaning we were through work) and the way he was moving, he thought I was on the engine. I knew I had to catch the engine, so I started running toward it. I made a flying leap for the grab irons on the front of the engine. From the speed of the train going east and me running full speed going west, my body swung straight out like a flag in a thirty- mile wind. My arms felt like they almost left my shoulders, but I did manage to hang on. When I got up in the cab I said, "Charlie, if you weren't a hillbilly, I'd whip you." He said, What's the matter?" I told him he had just stretched my arms about six inches longer than they should be trying to get back on the engine. We both had a good laugh, but my shoulders stayed sore for a long time.

1980s

Stuck Throttle

On November 12, 1983, Herb Ebert, a friend of mine, who also owned a Mooney airplane and I had flown in my plane down to Brazil, Indiana, a small town southeast of Terra Haute, Indiana. Every year a plane must be given an inspection (called Annual) by a licensed mechanic. We had been taking our planes to this particular mechanic for several years. The routine was to fly both planes down, leave one, and when it was finished, usually three days to a week later, fly down in the other plane, leave it and come back in the first one taken down. We had previously left mine, so on this particular occasion, we had taken his down and were flying back in mine. Though it was late afternoon the sun was still shining. I paid the mechanic, preflighted the plane, warmed up the engine, went through the check- list, and we started the take off roll east on the east-west runway. On take off, you are usually at full throttle until you have crossed over the end of the runway, or you are at approximately 400 feet above ground level. Then you reduce to climbing speed, that for the Mooney was 90 miles per hour. Everything went well until we reached the point where I attempted to reduce the throttle. It wouldn't reduce and we were wide open. To say the least, we were a little bit concerned. I turned, lined up with the runway and when I thought we could make the runway, shut the engine down and set up a glide for the field. Everything worked out, we landed, the mechanic made the necessary adjustments, and we were off for Peru.

Flying into Peru at night is a piece of cake. First you see the beacon light from Grissom Air force Base, which is approximately five miles south of Peru. As you pass over Grissom, at no less than 3000 feet, (they are a little testy about that and that is also government regulation), you see the huge flood lights that light up the hangars at Grissom. After passing Grissom, you start descending to 1500 feet, approaching altitude at Peru airport. Approximately six miles north of Grissom, on highway 31, at that time was a 76 truck stop with a huge, orange sign that was lighted. When you arrived over this sign, you turned due west and in approximately one mile, you arrived at the south end of the runway at Peru Airport. Flying at night is a different experience in a small plane. Usually at night, it is very smooth flying, as the wind is usually still. One night while flying north of Indianapolis, I could see the lights from "Indy", Kokomo, Marion, Wabash, Logansport, and Peru all at the same time.

A Winner

Dealing with animals on the railroad usually ends in disaster, at least for the animals, and unpleasant thoughts for the engineer. However, one day on a trip from Cincinnati to Peru in 1985, I had an encounter with a small dog that never knew the meaning of giving up. He should have been awarded a ribbon for his courage, determination, and will to live on this occasion. As we came around the curve at the bottom of the hill, coming into Peru, there were two small dogs on the track. I remember we had a rather long train but I don't remember if it was a freight train or coal train. When I blew the horn, they started running down the center of the track ahead of us. I had slowed the train to approximately thirty miles per hour, in anticipation of the twenty mile per hour slow order for the Wabash River Bridge. As we continually gained on them, I could see they were nice looking, well kept dogs. About a city block ahead where the track turned out over the bridge, there were several cottages so I figured, if they didn't get off before, they would get off at one of them. When we reached the curve that led onto the bridge, one of them did get off but the other continued around the curve and onto the bridge. On the bridge there were no stones between the ties only open cracks. At this time his forward motion would be stopped and he would have to start again. Added to this he was nearing exhaustion from running about a city block at full speed. We began to gain on him very rapidly now. There was a timber approximately eight to ten inches wide on the outer edge of the bridge. Evidently he thought we were about to overtake him, so he jumped over on this timber and kept running.

As we caught up to him, there was enough clearance for the front end of the engine to pass over him. However, just below my window, the fuel tank extended out over the timber he was running on. Momentarily, he was struck by the fuel tank, where he dropped twenty to thirty feet into the river below. As I looked back to see how he was doing, he came to the surface and began swimming furiously for shore. I wonder what he was thinking? Maybe, should he have stayed home today?

Canadian Fishing Trip

In 1985 my friend Herb Ebert asked me to go on a fishing trip to Canada. His idea was to take his plane, a four place Mooney, fly to Minnesota, cross the border at International Falls and land at an airport just beyond the border. There we would go through customs and then be picked up by a bush plane mounted on floats. Haley's Camp, the fishing lodge we would make reservations with, would furnish the plane. Haley's Camp was located some distance back in the bush on the English River. Jim McElheny, whom I had worked with years ago when cut off the railroad, would also be going along. Herb owned a machine shop and at the time, Jim was working for him. The morning we departed, I called weather for a weather briefing and though I didn't receive a severe clear report, it nevertheless looked like pretty good conditions for a VFR trip. We took off early from the local airport and headed north in a bright blue sky. West of Chicago we picked up some light scattered rain. While going through the rain I looked back to see how Jim who was sharing the back seat with some of our luggage and fishing equipment we couldn't get in the luggage compartment, was fairing the trip. Evidently the rain, or close quarters, wasn't bothering him for he was sound asleep. I've got a picture to prove it. After landing on the Canadian side, we went through customs, and then, after a short car ride, we loaded in the bush plane. Though it had been about forty years since I first flew a plane, this was a new experience for me as I had never flown or rode in a seaplane. The pilot, flying this plane, was the owner of the fishing camp. He had this plane and owned two others, and also had another pilot flying for him. The take off was fantastic and the landing was even better. Lakes were everywhere and the scenery was beautiful. I was really impressed. I told the pilot I was also a licensed pilot and asked if it would be possible for him to guide me through a few take offs and landings? He said, "Sure, we'll get together after supper." However, after supper he got a call to go pick up another load of fishermen, so my seaplane instruction was cancelled. We stayed in cabins and ate in a dining hall nearby.

The next morning we were up early and soon after, we were in the dining hall seated at long tables that were filled with good food. After breakfast, we were assigned a boat and a guide. The guides were Indians who lived in the area. Later, while talking to our guide, I asked him what the Indians in this area did for a living. He said," Most of them live off the government and a lot of them are alcoholics."

We had twenty pound test line and would be fishing mostly for Wall Eyes and Northern Pike. After going out about a half mile from camp, we stopped and threw out our lines. We were soon catching fish on both sides of the boat and all of them were big ones. I threw my line out once and got a strike as soon as it hit the water. With that one strike, my bait, hook, steel leader, and about three feet of twenty pound test line was gone. They do grow them big up there. At lunchtime, you pull into a clearing anywhere along the lake and the guides, who have brought cooking utensils and food from the camp along with some fish you have caught, prepare your lunch. About 3:30 in the afternoon, we would head back for camp and a short rest before supper. After a day of fishing, we had all the fish we wanted along with other choices of meat and all the trimmings.

Another day out in the boat, we were all putting mosquito repellent on for the mosquitoes were big and plentiful. I noticed the guide never used any. Thinking he might not be able to afford it, I asked if he would like to have some. He said, "No I don't need it." Come to think of it, I had never seen him swatting at them. I asked why they never bothered him? He said," If you use soap that doesn't have an odor, they won't bother you."

 On the last day out while we were fishing, Herb was running the boat and for some reason I had stood up. At this point in time, Herb hit a stump that was barely sticking out of the water. I almost went flying out of the boat. My fishing rod did. However, I managed to grab it before it went under. I understand hitting a stump where there are lots of stumps is no big deal, but in this lake of hundreds of acres this was the only stump in sight, and he hit it. I let him know I was not too impressed with his boat handling ability. I still remind him of it occasionally lest he forget.

 After three days of fishing all day, wee were ready to head home. We had all the fresh fish we wanted to eat while we were there, and we had a lot to bring home. The guides cleaned the fish and packed them in dry ice for the trip home.
Early the next morning after breakfast, we flew out in the bush plane. After landing and going through customs, we loaded up and pointed Herb's plane for Indiana. I would recommend this trip to anyone who likes to fish for this is fishing at its finest.

Black Angus

In 1986 our terminal where we reported for work had been moved to Chicago and I took a job that ran between Chicago and Columbus, Ohio. Sometime later we were on an eastbound freight around midnight and approximately forty to fifty miles north of Columbus, I could see something huge on the track ahead of me. In the early morning fog and darkness, I couldn't make it out .As we got closer; I could see it wasn't moving though I was blowing my horn. We were on straight track running about fifty miles per hour. When I saw it wasn't going to move, I dumped the air and at that same time, realized it was a herd of Black Angus cattle on both sides and in the middle of the track. I knew at that speed we would not get stopped and we didn't. We went right through the middle of them, and they never made a move. The brakeman, on the second unit, later told me he saw one of the cattle go flying up between the first and second units right in front of him. He said though it looked like a cow, he couldn't believe it was as he had never seen anything like that before. Usually when you hit a large animal, they go one side or the other, or they will go under the engine and stay there. It was upsetting to hit them for not only the cattle's sake but for whoever owned them. I could only imagine the money loss that would be involved.

 A few minutes after we stopped, I saw lights coming my way. They were headlights on Three Wheelers (the type ridden by kids but also used by hunters and farmers.) They pulled up to the engine and said they were looking for a heard of Black \Angus and wondered if we had seen them? I said, "Yes we sure did and we ran right through the middle of them." The one who turned out to be the owner said, "You are kidding me." I said, "Sir, I wish I was." That was a day I'm sure that farmer will never forget. He said one of his farm hands had left the gate unlatched and the cattle had gotten out.

A Bout With Hugo

A few years before I retired, my wife and I decided that after retirement, we would buy an RV Trailer and do some traveling. In 1986 my niece had a small travel trailer she wanted to sell and she suggested we buy it, take a few trips, and see if that was really what we wanted to do. We bought the trailer and while making one of those trips, we lost a cap off of one of the vents. A few days later, when I was going to the trailer sales to get the vent replacement, I asked my wife if she would like to ride along. That was a mistake for when we got back, we owned a new 33-foot RV. A trip we took with it in September 1989 proved to be rather unusual trip. We arrived at Myrtle Beech, South Carolina on September 19th late in the afternoon. At this time there was little concern about a Hurricane named Hugo away out in the ocean somewhere. The next morning there was more concern and by now it wasn't near as far out in the ocean. In fact it looked as if it might be heading for Myrtle Beech. As the day went on, the reports didn't get any better and the locals were getting quite concerned. I told my wife I didn't think there were more than about three main highways out of Myrtle Beech and if so, and if Hugo came in, those roads would be packed. That would be no place to be pulling a trailer, so we are leaving now. We pulled out and drove until we came to Sumpter. By this time it was dark and pouring rain. I pulled into a city parking lot and there we spent the night. It rained all night. The next morning, they said they thought Hugo would go up the coast so we drove inland to a state park. I talked to a man there and he told me he had just heard on the news that the wind in this area would be at least seventy miles per hour. As I have seen railroad cars turned over by wind, I told my wife I didn't think the trailer would stand a seventy-mile wind. We hooked up and headed for Columbia, South Carolina. We got there found a trailer park, and were getting set up when they reported the storm would be coming right through Columbia. We decided to head North and inland to get farther from the coast. My wife said, "Let's go to Charlotte we know it will never get that far inland." When we got in the area, she found a campground in the guide and we drove to the entrance of it. I said this doesn't look like a campground. It had a huge entrance gate and the buildings were big and expensive looking. Not what you usually see around the average campground. I pulled up to the entrance gate and asked the lady there if this was a campground? She said, "It sure is." After looking around, I told Pat I believe we are in Jim and Tammy Baker's place. I had recently seen some pictures of it in a magazine. I asked the lady at the gate if it was Jim Baker's place and she said it was. We were really impressed. It was a very nice place. It had its own enclosed shopping center. It was like walking down a street with stores on each side and a sky above you. There were nice homes and condos. Later that evening as I was setting up the trailer, Pat came out and said, "Jack, you are not going to believe this. They just said on the T. V. Hugo is coming through here. Where are we going now?" I said, "We are not going anywhere. We have run all day and every time we change directions Hugo changes too, so I'm not running anymore. This is it." Later the park sent a man around to the trailers who said there would be a bus later that would pick up everyone and take them to a community building. This building was beside a building of about fifteen stories that was under construction. I told Pat I wouldn't feel safe there. If the wind got strong enough, it might bring that unfinished building down. Anyway, I had already found a building I liked. It was an A Frame Restroom built out of cement with an outside layer of stone. If that building blew down, everything else would already be gone. We stayed in the trailer listening to the radio until about 3:00 AM. At this time they were saying the wind would soon be 70 mph and the worst was yet to come. With two chairs, a light and a portable radio, we left for the restroom. The rain was pouring, the wind was very strong, and the water was 3 to 4 inches deep on the ground. When we got in the restroom, the radio was missing. I went back looking for it and found it covered with water lying on the ground where I had dropped it. I shook the water out of it, dried it off, and it has continued to work to this day. The wind continued to pick up. Soon the trees started breaking off and the lights went out. I've always heard a storm like this, sounds like a freight train and that's absolutely right. The lights were off all night. When morning came, the wind had died down, so we ventured out. Ten to twelve inch trees had been snapped off from ten to twenty feet above the ground. Others were blown over from the ground up. Trees were down all over the park and roads were blocked, but no trailers were damaged. The closest I saw was where a tree had missed one by about eight inches. Later as we walked through the park, we saw where a lot of trees had been blown down on homes and condos in the park. I called Pirate Land, the park where we had been at Myrtle Beech, and they said, "Don't come back here, there's nothing left." We decided we would go to Panama City, Florida but we had to wait for three days for them to get the roads opened up. On the way to Panama City we blew a tire on the trailer. When I examined the other tires, I found big knots on the inside of two of them. When we got to Panama City, I went to a tire dealer and he agreed that the tires were defective. As he didn't have them in stock, we had to wait a couple days for them. We got the tires replaced and after being there three days, it was and had been raining continuously, so we decided it was time to go. Though we have had many nice trips in the trailer, this was not one of them.

The van and trailer my wife and I experienced Hurricane Hugo in.

Temptation

While working No. 300, at one time called The Fast Flying Virginia, from Chicago to Columbus, Ohio, we passed by a golf course on the south side of Chicago. Being a golfer, I knew how distracting a loud noise could be as you started forward with your club from the back swing. As I knew the exact time to blow the horn, I just couldn't resist the temptation. Believe me, there is nothing more distracting than a locomotive horn at close range. We would usually get a reaction, either in loud shouting, we couldn't understand above the roar of the engine, or a derogative gesture, we understood very well.

Columbus Zoo

While on layover, one afternoon in Columbus, Ohio, some of us guys decided we would go to the Columbus Zoo. Just to pass the time while we were waiting to be called. We had a car there at the motel we used for such occasions. After arriving at the zoo and after looking at some of the animals outside, we decided to go inside to look around. We soon came upon a large enclosure that housed a gorilla family. It consisted of a very huge male, a female, and a baby gorilla. The front of the enclosure was a wall made of glass about eight feet tall and about twelve to fourteen feet long. As we stood in front observing the gorillas, the female and the baby were sitting on the right and the male was sitting on the left. As we stood there along with the other onlookers, I saw one of our group standing in the middle of the glass making faces at the male. I also saw the male gorilla kept looking back at him. After a length of time, the male got up, walked over to the glass, and then started walking along beside the glass toward the right side of the enclosure. When he got to where our friend was standing, without even breaking his stride, he hit the glass with a thunderous blow right in front of our friend's nose. Our friend, along with the rest of us jumped backwards, thinking we had been had. After we regained our composure, we examined the glass to see how it ever with stood a blow of that magnitude. We could see it was very thick glass and lucky for us it was. I guess the moral to this story is; if you are not absolutely sure you are safe, don't monkey with the gorillas.

Open Cockpit

While on our yearly trip at Myrtle Beech, South Carolina, we were sitting on the beech when a red double wing, open cockpit airplane flew by. It immediately caught my eye for through all my years of flying, I had never flown in and open cockpit airplane. At one point in time back in the forties when I was still in high school, a plane like this one would do acrobatics over Hinton on pretty regular bases and every time he did I was glued to his every move. The next day the red plane was back making trips up and down the coast. I figured he must hauling passengers, as he wasn't pulling banners as the other planes were doing. I started asking questions around the area trying to find his base of operations. It wasn't long until I found him. He had a strip cut out of a pine grove just south of town. He had a small operations office there where I bought a ticket and waited for the plane to come back for my flight. It wasn't long before the plane reappeared making an approach to the field. After landing, the pilot walked into the office and the lady told him I was waiting for a flight. As we walked toward the plane, I asked the pilot if he would do some acrobatics during the flight? He said," No, I can't do that. If anything happened, my insurance would not be any good." I also told him I was a licensed pilot. When we got to the plane, he told me to get in the front seat, handed me a leather flying helmet, complete with goggles and earphones, checked my seat belt to make sure it was tight and then he climbed into the rear seat. He fired up the big radial and after a control and engine check, we were rolling. In a very short distance, with all that power, we were flying. We climbed to about 3000 feet, leveled out, and headed out over the ocean. After clearing the beech area, the nose suddenly went straight up. After ringing it out pretty good, he said, "OK, it's all yours do what you want." After I had flown for a while, he told me to head back for the strip. When we got within a couple miles of the strip, he took over and we went in for a perfect landing. After telling me we couldn't do acrobatics and then diving me straight for the ocean, I was quite excited and getting an opportunity to fly the plane was icing on the cake. I considered the money for that ride had been well spent for it had been a long time since I had enjoyed anything that much.

Building And Flying The Double Winger

I was talking to a friend of mine one day, Harry Denham, and I said, "Harry, why don't we build an open cockpit double winger?" He said," I have one already started. Why don't you help me build it? I said, "Sure, why not." Winter would be coming on soon but Harry has a huge building he calls the barn, that is a combination workshop and storage. It also has a huge upstairs room that would be warmer for the winter months so that was where we worked on it. After several months, the fuselage, wings, elevators, stabilizers, and rudder were completed and covered. Next came the painting, and attaching the wings to be sure they were properly aligned. Now the weather was getting a little warmer so we were ready to move downstairs. In order to do this the wings would have to be removed to get through the double doors and lowering it down to the ground floor would be a task in itself. In getting it down we used a tractor with a front-end loader to lower it. Once on the bottom floor, the wings had to be reattached, some controls hooked up, engine and cowling work, and several finishing touches. As it happened we had just finished the plane when near by Grissom Air Force Base was about to have its annual air show and they asked Harry if he would bring the plane out for a display. So we loaded it on a trailer, hooked Harry's truck to it, and with a police escort headed for the airbase. Harry was driving the truck and watching for clearances on his side, and I was checking clearances on the right side. There were a lot of things to look for as the wings far exceeded normal clearance. There were trees, posts, and signs to name a few. Well, we had just about made it. We were about fifty feet from turning into the air base when I saw this small road sign on my side. I told Harry but evidently he didn't hear me and before I could get him stopped, we clipped it. The right tip of the wing had been damaged. Enough to make any grown man cry, but not Harry, being the resourceful guy he is, he worked on it until it looked like new again in time for the show. We put it on display; put a big stuffed "Snoopy" with leather flying helmet and goggles in the cockpit. The plane was white, trimmed in bright red. The combination was quite a crowd pleaser.

Some weeks later we had it at the local strip we fly out of. At this time it was called Weed Field. While waiting to get it inspected by the FAA, we were making taxi runs up and down the runway to get an idea how the plane would handle. Soon afterwards the FAA inspected it and after a few more days of taxi experience and lifting the plane a few feet off the ground, Harry felt he was ready to give it a try. As I watched him on his take off run, the plane seems to lift off early in the take off run, but then it didn't seem to gain altitude very rapidly. There were trees at the end of the runway to be concerned with. He did make it over the trees but not by much. He climbed out but never did gain much altitude. When he landed he said the plane didn't seem to want to climb. We tried changing the angle of the elevators. This helped a little but not a lot. We changed to a different pitch propeller. Again this helped a little but not much. In the mean- time, I had gotten in a little more taxi time and while going down the runway and lifting off two to three feet, I suddenly realized I was about twenty feet off the ground and the trees at the end of the runway were coming up fast. I said to my self "OH Well" I shoved the throttle all the way open, pulled the stick back and went flying. The tree- tops were still above me, and I was beginning to wonder if I would make it. I found that in order to maintain altitude, I had to leave the throttle wide open. Not a good thing. We decided to try yet another prop of a different pitch. This helped more than the one before but was still not enough. The only thing left was to go to a higher horsepower engine. This was done and though I haven't flown it yet, since the change, Harry has and he says it flies like a different airplane.

Building an airplane is costly and very time consuming, to say the least, but it is a great deal of joy when completed. I would have to say Harry was the builder and I was the helper, though we did use some of my ideas. There is a lot of satisfaction in starting with an engine, glue, wood and fabric, putting it together, and then going flying in it. Should you decide to tackle this project, be forewarned, it takes lots of desire, know how, money, and an understanding wife.

Yours truly in front. Harry in back.

Finished product some months later.

End Of The Line

I soon realized that running from Chicago to Columbus instead of running from Peru to Cincinnati or Chicago, was a different kind of railroading. We had to drive approximately three and one half hours each way to and from Chicago, where we went on duty. There were five of us on the crew and we all rode together. Some of the other crews rode separately. I imagine that got a little expensive. Our running mileage on the railroad was practically doubled and the number of crossings we had to pass over was also practically doubled. Any time you pass over a crossing, you not only run the chance of connecting with an auto, but also big trucks, school buses, gas or gasoline trucks, anyone of which can ruin your whole day. Though I came close to hitting a school bus a few times, (the same school bus ran across in front of me twice during a trip through Muncie one day.) I was fortunate never to hit a gas or gasoline truck, though I did come close a few times. It's unbelievable how often someone will try to beat a train to a crossing. It is usually teenagers, someone who has had a few drinks, or someone who for some reason or another doesn't see the train. Sometimes they win, sometimes they lose. In case of a tie, the locomotive still wins. Having avoided any catastrophe I couldn't walk away from, in my forty years of service, I began to wonder if I was pressing my luck. Also at this time, the company was offering an early retirement. After much thought, I decided it was time to accept their offer. I knew I would miss my fellow employees, and at times, I would miss the railroad, for though a few times we didn't agree the pluses far out numbered the minuses, working for the C&O that later became Chessie System and finally CSX. I was well paid, thanks to our union, the locomotive Engineers, to do a job that was interesting, enjoyable, and at times, very exciting. Just one more time, with the sun and wind at my back, I would like to lean out the window of a 7400, look back and see 80 "Piggy Backs" behind me know there was a caboose on the rear end, and be westbound out of Cincinnati for Peru. That was railroading; those were the days.

Climbing aboard #300, from Chicago to Columbus,
Ohio for next to last trip before retirement.

Next to last trip on # 300 out of Chicago for Columbus, Ohio.

Peru Depot as it looks today.

Glossary

1. Highball--Signal for train to depart.
2. B of I --Board Of Inquiry.
3. Manifest-------------------------------------- Train consisting of high revenue freight.
4. Ribbon Rail------------------Rail that has been welded together to form long lengths.
5. Covered Wagon----------------A cab over type road diesel made by General Motors.
6. Pool Jobs-----------A list of crews who would work first in, first out, over a given territory.
7. Assigned Jobs----- Crews on these jobs were called at approx. the same time each trip and on the same days of the week.
8. Third Brakeman-------An extra brakeman that was called for a train that exceeded 69 cars.
9. Extra Board------------A list from which men were called for extra trains or to fill vacancies of regular men.
10. Stoker---------- A steam operated auger that transferred coal from the tender to the firebox.
11. Tender------- ---That part of a steam engine where coal and water were stored for use during operation.
12. Drivers--- Driving wheels of a steam engine.
13. K 2s---------- Steam engines built by American Locomotive Works (Alco) used on the Chicago Division in 1100 series.
14. K3s------------Steam engines built by Alco, used on the Chicago Division in the 1200 and 1300 series
15. Hostler-------- A locomotive fireman who moves engines in and around the round house, diesel house and ready track for engines to be worked on or serviced.
16. Messenger Service- ------When a locomotive fireman is called to ride a dead engine that is being pulled in a train. (sometimes the air brakes would set up on these dead engines, while in route, and the fireman would have to release them.)
17. Operator---------------An employ who copies train orders from the dispatcher and delivers them to the engine and train crews.
18. Frog--------------------------- That part of a track that connects two intersecting rails.
19. Blue Light-----A blue light or flag placed at the head end of a track on which there is equipment being serviced or worked on. This track cannot be entered until blue light is removed by one of the workman.
20. Leave Of Absence------------ Permission to leave the railroad employment to go to service, school etc. The employee may return at a later date without loss of seniority.
21. Caboose- Usually placed at the end of a train for the conductor and flagman to ride in to keep surveillance of the train.
22. Train order------------------An order, put out by the dispatcher to train and engine crews.
23. Wash out---------- A violent horizontal signal with a flag or light given on or near the track indicating stop immediately.
24. Steady-------------------- a slow horizontal movement of hand or light meaning to proceed at a very slow speed.

25. Proceed--- Vertical movement of hand or light.

26. Pat On the stomach   --Go to lunch.

27. Horn or Whistle Signals:

      2 shorts – proceed.

      3 shorts—back up.

      2 longs, 1short & 1 long-------------------------------- signal for highway crossing.

28. Derailment-------------- when any rolling stock, engines, cars etc. have left the rail.

29. Derail------- A device used to intentionally cause a derailment. Used to prevent cars or other equipment from fouling main line or other tracks.

30. Crummy-- another name for caboose.

31. Carrying Signals---Approaching engine carrying green signals, indicating there will be another section of that train following or approaching engine carrying white signals indicating he was called as an extra train.

GM # 6299

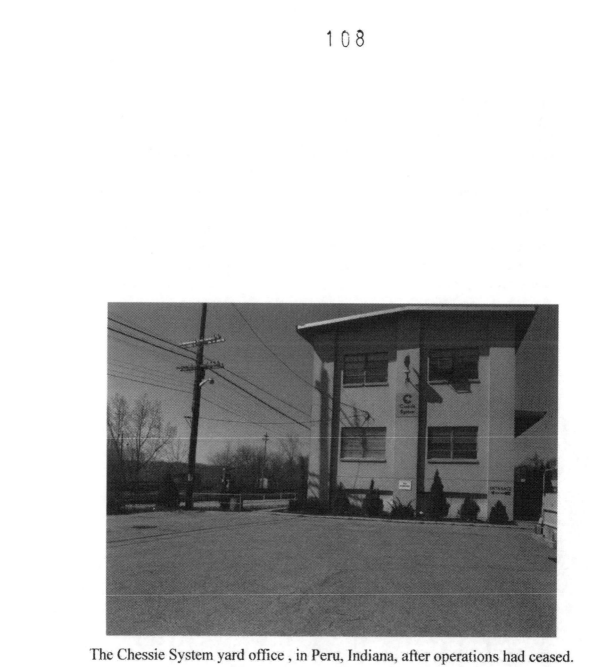

The Chessie System yard office , in Peru, Indiana, after operations had ceased.

Printed in the United States
by Baker & Taylor Publisher Services